FINGERPRINTS *of a* LOVING GOD

SUZANNE M PHIPPS

WESTBOW
PRESS®
A DIVISION OF THOMAS NELSON
& ZONDERVAN

Scripture taken from the Holy Bible, NEW INTERNATIONAL VERSION®.
Copyright © 1973, 1978, 1984 by Biblica, Inc. All rights reserved worldwide.
Used by permission. NEW INTERNATIONAL VERSION® and NIV® are
registered trademarks of Biblica, Inc. Use of either trademark for the offering
of goods or services requires the prior written consent of Biblica US, Inc.

WestBow Press books may be ordered through booksellers or by contacting:

WestBow Press
A Division of Thomas Nelson & Zondervan
1663 Liberty Drive
Bloomington, IN 47403
www.westbowpress.com
1 (866) 928-1240

Because of the dynamic nature of the Internet, any web addresses or
links contained in this book may have changed since publication and
may no longer be valid. The views expressed in this work are solely those
of the author and do not necessarily reflect the views of the publisher,
and the publisher hereby disclaims any responsibility for them.

Any people depicted in stock imagery provided by Thinkstock are models,
and such images are being used for illustrative purposes only.
Certain stock imagery © Thinkstock.

ISBN: 978-1-5127-0783-0 (sc)
ISBN: 978-1-5127-0784-7 (hc)
ISBN: 978-1-5127-0782-3 (e)

Library of Congress Control Number: 2015913198

Print information available on the last page.

WestBow Press rev. date: 10/30/2015

Contents

Dedication

To all those who journey from broken-heartedness to wholeness by God's great love and mercy.

To all those who journey alongside those who are hurting and who celebrate the miracle of healing in their lives.

Acknowledgements

There are many people I would like to acknowledge.

I give my heartfelt thanks to my husband, Paul. Thank you for being the amazing man that you are and for your incredible support throughout my writing process. You didn't even flinch when I told you that I believed God was directing me to write a book about my story. You are truly a wonderful man. I am ever so pleased that you asked me to marry you – and that I said yes! Thanks, darling, for the very best chapters of my life.

Thanks to Abby and Rory for your support throughout the writing process. You coped very well with the "project" going on around you, especially when you knew that there were conversations being had on the side that you were not a party to! I love you both very much, and I am ever so proud of what amazing young people you are.

Thanks also to Peter Griffiths for your support, wisdom, great skill, and tremendous sense of humour. I must say that the sense of humour was absolutely vital! Thank you for always believing that I would work my way through the process and that there was a wonderful, healthy life waiting for me on the other side.

Thanks to my mum and dad. I know that I put you "through the mill", but your love for me was consistent throughout. You have always reminded me that the work was worth doing – and worth doing well. Thanks.

Thanks to Don and Ruth Ferguson, a truly remarkable couple and a God-given blessing in both difficult times and the best of times. I still miss your wisdom and honest communication, Ruth. I am looking forward to a reunion with you when our Father calls me home.

Thanks to Romy. You have been a great friend through a very difficult season of my life. I only wish that you lived closer to me!

Thank you, Lorraine Stacey, for your support and practical help in my earlier stages of writing this book. You were very generous with your feedback, support, and practical help. Thank you very much.

Mohammad, Rosemary, and Karelia, I will always be grateful for your timely help and wisdom. Unfortunately, the intervening years have made it impossible for me to track you down. Nonetheless, your input in my life was enormous and significant.

Author's Note

The name of the person referred to as Daniel in this book has been changed out of respect for his family.

The name of Mr Black has also been changed. My apologies to any other Mr Blacks!

Preface

It is a very brave thing to write a book. It is even braver to write a book about yourself. It assumes that there is something about your life that is worth writing about. It assumes that others might be interested in your story. It assumes that you have the skills necessary to take your own history and put it onto paper.

My story is one of walking through the trauma of abuse at the hands of a schoolteacher, through days of silence into days of confronting all that was "haunting" me. And yet moving beyond that into days of healing and wholeness.

I remember some days of intense frustration. I was slogging my way through counselling as I tried to work through all that had happened to me. They were days where I felt I was going round and round in circles. Days where things felt pretty bleak. Days where I had little hope but relied heavily on the hope of others. I felt so very stuck.

In those days, I went searching for books to read. I yearned for a book that told a story similar to mine, but I wanted a book with chapters to show that there was a way through this nightmare and that there might even be better days ahead. Alas, I could find no such book. I could find books written about abuse that were written by professionals and although these were excellent books, I felt no heart connection at all with the texts. It felt like a bit of a gap in what

I needed. So I hope that I have written the book that I wanted – indeed, needed – in those days.

I'm not at all sure that writing a book was ever really my idea. Over the years, a number of people have said to me in passing, "I think you should write a book." The first few times, I dismissed the suggestion quickly, but after a while I began to wonder if there was something in their comments. The idea lay dormant for some time. Then it seemed that each time I opened the Scriptures, there was something about "writing it all down" or about "remembering the past and all that God has done." Eventually, I shared my thoughts with my husband, Paul. I expected him to chuckle or, at the very least, not to take me seriously. I was surprised to find him very supportive of the idea and of my ability to do it.

Still, the idea lingered at the back of my mind. Suddenly circumstances changed, and I found that I had more time on my hands. With a little more prompting from the Holy Spirit (and my husband), I started to write.

I truly hope that this book will fill in that gap. I pray that in reading my story contained within these pages, others will catch a glimpse of the hope that God places in our hearts. I pray that there is assurance that our God is not distant but is interested in all of the details of our lives. We really can see the Divine's fingerprints over all of the events of our lives. Know that God makes good come out of even the terrible.

Introduction

The sun spills in through the windows of a classroom.

A Sunday school class of ten-year-olds are intent on the lady speaking at the front. One or two of the boys wriggle just a little.

In the middle of the group of children are two girls sitting side by side. They share the occasional glance at each other and the occasional smile. They are friends. Most weeks, they only see each other at Sunday school and church. Still, they know there will be time for chatting when Sunday school is finished for today. Then there will be some Katie and Suzanne time.

In height, the two girls are very similar. Both have light brown hair. Katie's is shorter (it sits on her shoulders), while Suzanne's is longer. Katie is more outgoing than Suzanne. Suzanne is quieter than Katie but that doesn't bother them.

They have so much in common. They are loved daughters being raised in Christian homes. They attend their local primary schools and both are fairly bright. Neither of them is fussed on sport!

Both Katie and Suzanne have made decisions to invite Jesus into their lives.

A look passes between them. They giggle quietly as they share the humour of something that has been said.

When we flash forward a bit, we see that life has become very different for these girls. At twenty-five years of age, the girls are now women, women who walked rather different paths.

Katie is a well-rounded young woman. She has held good jobs. She is newly married and is happily setting up home with her loving husband. She is excited about the prospect of starting a family soon. In the meantime, the couple are enjoying an active social life. Katie's life has seen much blessing, and her challenges have been small. Yet her faith wanes.

Suzanne has had a very different life experience. At twenty-five, she is working hard to put her life in order and to heal her mind, soul, and body. Her life was altered by the behaviour of someone who crossed her path a number of years earlier. One year of exposure to this man has taken a toll – isolation, loss of confidence, self-doubt, lack of hope, and ill health. She has planned suicide.

There have been positives in Suzanne's life as well. She has built a great career, she has made some great friends, and her faith has stayed sure. Now her faith grows stronger still.

The two lovely little girls have grown into women. They were friends in childhood and still are friends in adulthood.

I know these girls. In fact, I am Suzanne in the story.

Becoming Kiwis

I was born in the late sixties in a northern England industrial town called Oldham. My parents had been high-school sweethearts who married young. I was born when they had been married for just over a year.

My mother, at that point, was a student nurse just months from sitting her state finals and my arrival interrupted those plans. My dad was a sheet-metal engineer at that stage of his life.

I was fortunate to be blessed with a caring family who loved me and who sought to do the very best that they could for me.

I was followed two years later by a brother called Simon. It must be said that I always adored my brother and I was exceedingly loyal and protective of him. The poor boy must have frequently felt that he had two mothers!

My earliest memories, from when I was three years old, are lovely ones. Surprisingly, I have quite a number of memories from that time.

At that point, my family was living in a two-up two-down in an industrial town in the north of England. Having seen the house as an adult, I can appreciate that it was a little home, but as a small child I can remember bumping down the mountain of stairs on my bottom in what I thought was a big house.

I remember my maternal grandmother's house almost as well as my own which is not surprising given that I spent a lot of time in her home. I remember standing on a chair and wearing an apron to "help" her wash the dishes. Grandma had a great love of mints (particularly Mint Imperials) and would always have some in her bag or on the mantle. She would give me one with a warning not to tell Mum or "we'd both be in trouble." I thought that Grandma was great. When I was a small child, I knew that she thought I was great too.

It must be noted that my maternal grandmother could be a formidable woman. She was certainly not afraid of a battle or of going in to defend a principle. My parents tell the story of being away on holiday with Grandma and visiting a local butcher. She asked the price of some meat and voiced her disapproval when the butcher told her how much he expected for it. She told him that she would never pay that much for it back home. He promptly asked how much she usually paid and sold it to her at that price. To me, my grandmother was kind, fun, and always generous. There was never any doubt at all that she loved me and that she would always be in my corner.

There was a little boy named Ian who lived next door to my family. Ian and I were a similar age. Ian would climb over the fence between our homes to come and play. He was much more adventurous than I was, and always seemed to be getting into mischief. He was fun to play with, although he shocked me at times.

When I was three, my family took a trip to Blackpool in our little Fiat Bambina. It was in the days before children were required to travel in safety seats. I stood as tall as I could on the back seat of the car, with my head up through the open sunroof, in order to get the best possible view of the "luminations". The lights sparkled like millions of stars. The gentle breeze through my hair and the smell of the ocean made it all seem magical.

The late sixties and early seventies were difficult years in the north of England with mass redundancies and high unemployment. Life was becoming more difficult. My parents made the courageous decision to emigrate. Initially, they thought of going to Australia, in particular to Sydney, as my mother had extended family there.

Around that time, however, the New Zealand government was actively recruiting skilled workers. The New Zealand government instituted a great scheme whereby it paid most of the financial costs of a worker's relocation, in exchange for a bond period of two years' work for the company that offered him or her employment. It was a focused programme that was offered to workers who had particular skills. My father had skills that the New Zealand government was keen to attract.

For my parents, it was to be a great start to their adventure. They thought to stay in New Zealand for two years and then move across the Tasman Sea to Sydney, Australia. Originally, we were to go to Invercargill, but later this was changed to Christchurch.

The wheels were put into motion. Applications were made and passports were obtained. I remember visiting various family members and friends to say farewell. After making our tearful goodbyes, our family of four boarded a plane to make the very long flight to the other side of the world.

It was a very long flight called the "milk run". It acquired its name because it made frequent stops on the way to New Zealand. Most of the stops were very brief. Sometimes, we passengers disembarked and were able to enjoy a run around. In other places, we were required to stay on the plane.

I guess that in 1971 it was more unusual for families with young children to be travelling such a distance. The airline staff were helpful and attentive. There were colouring-in books and crayons, which I was very impressed with. For at least some of the flight, there were plenty of spare seats. I remember being given a row of seats to sleep on. The armrests were pushed back so that, with a pillow and a blanket, it made a great bed for a little girl.

We arrived in Christchurch, New Zealand, on April 20, 1971. It was a beautiful, sunny day. Late April in Christchurch really is the middle of autumn, but April 20 was a lovely, warm day. It seemed to me, upon arriving in this new city, that there was very little there. We had flown into so many cities on our way, mostly large international cities, and Christchurch seemed so very small as we flew over it.

The airport was another surprise. At that time, it was very basic. I wondered where all the people were.

We were met at the airport by a man from the engineering firm that my dad was to work for. When I close my eyes, I can still picture this man. He wore shorts with long knee-high socks. I had never seen anyone dressed like that before! He was friendly and welcoming but I couldn't understand much of what he was saying.

We put all of our luggage into his car. I was so impressed with his station wagon. It was huge, or so it seemed to me. Even more impressive to me was the back window of the car, which had a handle to wind it down. I thought that was so cool.

My parents were exhausted and in need of sleep. Unfortunately for them, my brother and I had slept very well on the plane and were not so keen to head to bed. Added to that, it was to be my birthday on the following day. We all went birthday shopping before any unpacking and with our feet barely on the ground. My gift was a doll's pram to replace the one left back in England.

The town that we had left in the United Kingdom was set on hills, but our new city was largely on the flat. It seemed that all the houses had gardens, many of which were very pretty. We walked everywhere and gradually started to get our bearings. There were so many parks and so many trees. Even the sky looked different. For a start, the sky was blue more often than it was in our part of England!

It must have all been extremely unsettling for my parents and a difficult adjustment, especially for my mum. Dad was able to meet and get to know other people through work, but Mum was much more isolated at home with two small children.

It was a period of immigration for New Zealand, so there were a number of other English people who had also moved to Christchurch recently – some from the north of England, like us. A strong camaraderie developed within the group as they adjusted to a new lifestyle in New Zealand. There were day trips together as we all became familiar with our new surroundings.

For us as a family, things continued to be a little unsettled for a while. There were a few changes in homes in the first little while.

My parents were committed to their new life in New Zealand and to settling in well. As part of that commitment, we made a concerted effort to get to know the locals and to become more familiar with the Kiwi way of doing things. Even so, we did stick out like sore thumbs!

Following our move to Linwood (in the eastern suburbs of Christchurch), I was enrolled at the local kindergarten.[1] Oh how I loved kindy. As a four-year-old, I attended five mornings a week as preparation for starting school. I thought that kindy was a magical place. There were all sorts of things to play with and great adventures to be had. And everything was made with little children in mind! Even the toilets and basins were at my height.

Along one wall of the building there were massive French doors, which were flung wide open on most days to allow free movement inside and outside. As you went out the doors there was a massive decking area with a large veranda over top, which meant that even on damp, wet days, you could still play outside.

In the middle of the outside playground, there was a massive tree which provided shade for most of the outside area. From one of its strong branches hung a rope attached to a large, old tyre. It was a wonderful swing and three or four of us could easily share the ride.

At kindy, I learnt to speak Kiwi. I very quickly became aware that I had different words to name things or to express my thoughts. So wellies became gumboots, lorries became trucks, and so on. I became very adept at speaking Kiwi at kindy and speaking English at home.

As well as my attending kindy, there were other changes to our family life during this time. When she was a teenager, my mother

---

[1] In New Zealand a kindergarten is a preschool education network that caters for children generally between the ages of two years and four years of age. It is a mix of age appropriate activities. There is some free play time when the children choose which activity they would like to do and then a little more formal time where there is a story and a song or poem. When I was little the younger children would attend 3 afternoons a week and the older children (nearer to starting school) would attend 5 mornings a week.

had attended a Billy Graham crusade meeting and had responded to the call to commit her life to God. In her later teens, she laid that decision aside. During my family's first year in New Zealand, things had started to stir in Mum's heart again. About a year after immigrating, she reconfirmed her commitment to God.

A Walk into Faith

For me as a small child, the biggest change was the change to our family routine. We started attending church on Sunday mornings. Initially, it was just Mum and I who would go together. Later on, we all went as a family. I was somewhat put out about being taken to Sunday school when Dad and Simon were allowed to stay home.

The church was a Methodist church and the building seemed very old to me. It also seemed that it was always cold.

The Sunday school was held in a large hall, a multipurpose hall that was used for Sunday school on a Sunday but for badminton and all sorts of other things during the week. It was large, and it echoed. Every noise seemed to be amplified. In the winter, it was colder but I did like Sunday school.

The lady who was the teacher was very kind to me and always made me feel so welcome. I always enjoyed the Bible stories that she told us. They seemed to be so real. and I often found myself thinking about them later. I loved the songs that the teacher taught us. In particular, I enjoyed learning "Jesus Loves Me this I know for the Bible tells me so." I pondered the words at length and often wondered whether that could really be true? I gradually became aware that it is possible to have a relationship with this Jesus that they talked about and an interest and hunger developed in my heart and mind. My ears would prick up at the mention of the name Jesus.

I was drawn to learn as much about him as I possibly could. My introduction to Jesus had begun.

My dad became a Christian about a year after my mum had recommitted her life to God. It seemed to me at the time that we were going to church more and more.

There were other decisions and further adjustments made to our lives in New Zealand. My parents, decided to commit to staying in New Zealand for a bit longer and decided to build a house. This was an exciting adventure! But it was one that tightened the family finances further.

At this point, my mum took a job as a Nurse Aid[2] on a Geriatric Ward. The job was for two shifts at the weekends, which meant that my mum could work while my dad was at home able to care for Simon and me. It was a large commitment for Dad, but from a child's perspective it was great to have Dad's attention at the weekends. Looking back, it also left a lasting legacy for both Simon and me in terms of a great relationship with both of our parents.

Now there was also work on the house. My parents tried to keep the costs of building down as much as possible. One way they were able to accomplish this was by doing the interior decorating themselves. There were other ways. For one project, my parents had chosen a cream brick for the exterior of the house. The brick was solid and came flat on all sides but my parents wanted a more textured look so my dad spent hours with a hammer and a chisel, bevelling one side of each of the bricks. Simon and I were the "helpers", carrying

---

[2] A Nurse Aid in the 1970s was generally a member of staff on the ward who was either untrained or had little training who would work alongside trained staff (and under their supervision). They assisted with duties such as changing beds, showering patients, feeding patients and more general duties in the ward. They were important and indispensable members on the team.

bricks from one pile to another. I am sure that we were less helpful than we thought!

We loved spending time at the house as it was built. At that stage, there were some houses on the other side of the road, but there were few on our side and certainly none behind us. There were no fences around our house, so there was plenty to investigate. All around our new home, other houses were being constructed and roads were still being put in place. There was something new to look at each time we visited.

To me, our new home could have been a palace. In reality, it was a simple house but I loved it, and it was a home. I had my own bedroom, and I enjoyed a space that was mine.

When we first moved in, we had polished Rimu floors with the cost of carpet being deferred to a later date. Simon and I loved those floors. The lengths of wood worked beautifully as roads in our imaginary games that employed his Matchbox cars, our Lego, and a great deal of imagination.

Our teachers commented that we were both very quiet and found the noise of other children to be stressful. Our quietness might have been attributable to the floors that would echo any noise that we made. We had learnt to be quiet.

It took some time for neighbours, fences, and even footpaths to appear. I learnt to ride a bike without trainer wheels along the sand that was the footpath. This I know – the advantage of learning on sand is that if you fall off, the sand provides a soft landing, but the disadvantage is that it is very easy to fall off a bike while trying to ride on sand!

On my fifth birthday, I started school at the local state Primary School. Primary school was not like kindy and I was definitely not enamoured with school. By all accounts, I cried every day for the first year, at being left at school. I remember hating school. There was far too much work to be done and certainly not enough time for play.

In New Zealand, children start school on or close to their fifth birthday, wherever it falls in the year. This meant that there was always a trickle of children starting and it also meant that you might be the only one starting on any given day or week.

I think that starting school was always going to be an adjustment for me but it was made more difficult by the actions of a classmate. My teacher for New Entrants had this lovely way of helping the new children to settle. She would buddy up a new student with one of the other children who had been at school a little while.

Unfortunately in my case, my buddy was something of a bully. She was very mean. She teased me, called me names, embarrassed me in front of everyone else, and took to hiding my things. She liked having someone to boss around and it must be said at this point that she would boss everyone around if she possibly could. She did not restrict herself to me or even to children smaller than herself.

She would control everything that I did. Where I sat at lunchtime, whom I was allowed to play with, what I was allowed to play with, and even when I was allowed to go to the toilet in the breaks (this alone led to much embarrassment when I had "accidents"), which certainly did not help my confidence. There was name-calling. Even worse than that, she helped herself to things to eat from my lunch box.

I remember standing in line one day. The bell had rung and we then had to line up outside the classroom. On that occasion, I had made it to the classroom quickly and was second in line. She arrived and loudly announced to one and all that I was not allowed to be at the front of the line and would have to go to the back. I was too slow to move, so she dragged me to the end of the line by my collar. There were murmurs of protest from my classmates, but no one was brave enough to stand up to her.

I was a quiet child who became even quieter. My buddy was sneaky. Because I was quiet, everything went under my teacher's radar. My teacher remained completely unaware of what was going on.

I started having nightmares at night, which caused my parents some concern. I remember my mum having a talk with the teacher, who asked me if I was being bullied. At the age of five, I had no idea what that meant, so I failed to share the information that would have cast light on the situation. She asked me if anyone was hitting me or kicking me. I said no because my buddy didn't do those things. It was some years before I could put any real name on the behaviour, let alone try to deal with it. It must be said that it was a very different era. Bullying was not really recognised or identified as a problem.

Over time, the situation settled down but unfortunately it all left me rather wary of my peers. I enjoyed my own company all the more.

As a family, we developed some amazing friends during this time, largely through church contacts. These friends were different. They became like a new extended family. The bonds were firmer, and contact was regular. These were lovely, relaxed relationships. We were gathered in as additions to their own extended families.

There were moments when I wondered if they simply felt sorry for us but in reality, however, the friendships were sincerely and warmly extended. It was enjoyed by all.

We had settled into a local Methodist church. I think that this was largely because Mum's teenage church home had been Methodist. I enjoyed the Sunday school. My picture of God became clearer.

The 1970s was an interesting period for the church in Christchurch and, indeed, for churches throughout New Zealand. It was a period of time when there was a real hunger to see the Holy Spirit active in local churches (and the community). There was an amazing movement of the Holy Spirit which has been referred to by many as the "Charismatic Renewal".

I was a young child then, but I still remember the excitement that the Renewal brought to churches. As a child, I was aware that church was more exciting and lively, but I was also aware that not everyone was comfortable with the way the Holy Spirit was at work in the church. There was polarisation between different denominations. Even more sad was the polarisation between churches within the same denomination – e.g. one Methodist (or Baptist, etc.) church would take a different stance from another. Even amongst members of our own church, there was a polarisation in people's views and reactions.

A number of the congregants in my church became increasingly interested in the Baptism in the Holy Spirit. My own parents were amongst those who had a growing desire to see the Holy Spirit move in and touch their lives. I was young, but I was interested in the conversations that were going on around me. I saw first-hand and up close the amazing works that the Holy Spirit had done. I saw people speaking in tongues, I saw people "falling over in the Spirit", I saw people being healed, and, most of all, I saw people's lives being dramatically changed.

Over the course of time, I came to a point where I knew God to be real. I felt such an excitement to be in places where there was an amazing sense of the presence of God. I prayed at Sunday school and at home. I continued to soak up all that I could about God.

In our own home, my parents were eager to see more of God at work. They were baptised in water and also baptised in the Holy Spirit. They were so very hungry and thirsty for God, they sought out every opportunity to meet with his people.

For a season, we attended the Methodist church in the morning and then the New Life Centre in the evening, which meant that we all had a nap on Sunday afternoons. My parents were committed to the Methodist church and to seeing God move there, but they were also thirsty for more.

The New Life Centre at that point was a "church" of several hundred people. Many were like us, going to their denominational church in the morning and then going to the New Life Centre in the evening.

It was an amazing place to be. I remember the "buzz". And the place did buzz with hundreds of people who were excited to be in church. The music and the worship were very different from what I was accustomed to, and yet I was not at all surprised by it. We sang hymns and engaged in subdued worship in the mornings. This was followed by choruses, dancing, and loud singing in the evenings. It was a traditional church building in the morning and then a public hall in the evening.

The New Life Centre was full of people of all ages, but there were dozens of families there in the evenings. Along the back of the hall, there would be a line of trestle tables. Underneath them would be small children in sleeping bags with pillows, tucked down to sleep. There was a terrible noise one night when one of the tables collapsed on the sleeping children underneath. There was no injury to the children, but the crash certainly gave everyone a start!

New Life Centre would hold a Christmas convention each year. It started on Boxing Day and went through to New Year's Day. In the first year we attended, it was a live-in "camp" held in the halls of residence at Lincoln University, an incredible setting in the park-like grounds.

It really was complete madness for the week. Hundreds and hundreds of people gathered together in one place to celebrate God. There were lots of meetings and also so much fun and laughter. There was an amazing kid's programme that I was excited about. I learnt much that week. The lovely leader I had was so gentle and patient with all of us children. She was my hero. I adored her.

There are moments from that week that stand out even after all this time. The first was a baptism service held in the outdoor swimming pool. It was noteworthy because it seemed to me that there were a lot of people baptised that day. It was a beautiful, sunny day but even more than that, it was a powerful service with so many prophecies spoken into the lives of individuals. People would enter the water, give a brief testimony, be prayed for, be baptised, and be prophesied over. Before long, there were a number of people just floating in the pool, enjoying the presence of God. Meanwhile, the leaders would continue with the baptisms.

The second event that stands out was a wedding. In the middle of all the services, there was a beautiful wedding. I was allowed to go and watch! It was amazing. I was suitably impressed. In time, the couple would become great family friends.

I remember that the rather busy boy in the room across the hall would get up to mischief – like sliding down the banisters at great speed.

My parents persevered for some time with their dual allegiances. My father served at the Methodist church by teaching in the Sunday school. He even taught me. He was really rather good! But the time came when my parents believed it was time to make the New Life Centre our church home. They were honourable in their decision and in the communicating of that decision. My memory is that they seemed relieved once the decision had been made.

The first time that Simon and I attended the Sunday school at the New Life Centre was like stepping into a completely different country.

At this stage, New Life Centre met in the Horticultural Hall in Durham Street, but the Centre owned a building in Litchfield Street that provided rooms for Sunday school and so on. I was very nervous even to enter the building. Just beyond the entryway was a large staircase that led up to the first floor. From the entry, you could not see what was waiting upstairs for you. There were lots of other kids racing up. There were many children – it seemed like hundreds to me. The room was packed. Simon and I quietly took seats near the back. I felt like a fish out of water.

This Sunday school was called "Children's Church". The thinking was that it should be just like church for kids, a service like the grown-ups would be having, with all of the same trademarks. Children's Church would start with praise and worship. It was an amazing time with children raising their hands and their voices in worship. It was new and somewhat foreign to me and yet at the same time, it was rather like coming home.

There was a change to the Christmas convention format, which meant that a series of meetings were held at a similar time of the year and in the centre of Christchurch at the Horticultural Hall. Over the next few years, a variety of guest speakers were invited. There was always a special service on New Year's Eve. There would be an ordinary service followed by supper and then an enormous Praise Party. There was a great party atmosphere. Many of the chairs were pushed back to make room for dancing. Such an amazing mix of people – Pentecostals, Baptists, Methodists, Catholics, and

Anglicans, young and old, couples and singles – all celebrating together.

The year that Pastor Clark Taylor spoke was a special one for me. In one of the evening meetings, he preached about the story of Joshua and the walls of Jericho. I had a new Bible with me that I was reading, but Clark Taylor was a passionate and funny speaker, I would read a little and then listen to what he was saying.

He illustrated Joshua and the Israelites walking around the city of Jericho by marching around the pulpit. He talked about God pulling down the walls in our lives – the strongholds that hold us back. It was very evangelistic that evening. At the end of the sermon, he prayed and invited people forward who wanted to ask Jesus to enter their hearts. He explained that someone would pray with them.

It was like an arrow to my heart. I knew that I needed to make a decision. I remember thinking ever so clearly that if I died that day, then I would not be going to heaven. It was equally clear to me that, more than anything, I wanted to go to heaven.

The church musicians played some songs, and the congregation joined in but there in amongst hundreds of people, I felt alone with my thoughts and feelings. My head was all in a whirl as I thought about what the preacher had said. I understood that I did not have the relationship with God that I needed to have and that God wanted me to have. I knew without a shadow of a doubt that I wanted to go to heaven and that I wanted to invite Jesus into my heart. I knew these things with such clarity. My heart was desperate to respond.

I nudged my mum and said that I wanted to go forward. She looked a little puzzled and said that she thought that I didn't really need to go forward as I was already a friend of Jesus. I insisted that I did need to. She nudged my dad and told him, "Your daughter wants to go up. Can you take her up?" Dad was happy to oblige.

The hall was packed with people and I was a little nervous, but I was determined that I needed and wanted to do this, so I held firmly to my dad's big, rough hands as we made our way forward.

Once my dad and I were at the front, Clark Taylor prayed with all who had come forward as a group. Then we were invited to move to another room while the service continued. We were each paired up with someone to pray with us. These people also shared more information with us. I was the last person to be paired off. I remember being a little frustrated, thinking I was not being taken seriously enough!

I resolved in my own heart and mind that I was serious and that this was going to be a decision that I would always remember. That evening, I asked Jesus to be my Saviour and I invited him to be Lord of my life. Max Palmer (on the pastoral staff at the New Life Centre) prayed with me and gave me a booklet to read through. He was kind and explained things to me a little more. He told me that my life would never be the same again. He was certainly right about that!

I knew with absolute certainty that things had changed that night. It was a moment of great clarity for me. Even then, I understood the implications of my decision.

Did it make any difference to my day-to-day life? Yes. I was even more eager to learn and, more importantly I was eager to talk with God.

Innocence Lost

Life at school continued to tick along. I made friends with a small group of girls in my class. We tended to keep to ourselves and enjoy our own company. I loved to read, but I hated maths – not very unusual.

My school reports show me as a quiet student who was lacking in confidence. With a birthday late in April, I was frequently the youngest in the class or very near to it. At times, this was obvious! I was the last kid in the class to start to lose my baby teeth. And when it came to sport, I was always slower than everyone else. I felt clumsy in ball games and dreaded anything sporty.

As time went on, the differences between Simon and me became apparent. He was more socially adept, more sporty, and generally more confident. I became aware of people comparing us. In these comparisons, I seemed to come up short.

Contact with family in England was sporadic. My maternal grandmother would send letters and parcels, which were always very exciting. Phone calls were an unusual event because of the cost of them at that time.

When I was seven, my mother's cousin came to New Zealand on holiday. My mum was an only child who had been raised closely with her cousins, even living together with them until she was five years old. As an extension of that, her cousin was Uncle Bill to Simon and me. His visit was so exciting and much anticipated.

A plan was put in place. We would hire a camper van and travel around a large part of the South Island.

Uncle Bill was so cool! He was kind and fun. He would tease us both. We all laughed so much. Almost as soon as he arrived, I started to dread his leaving again. It was a fabulous holiday. We saw the amazing South Island with its quintessential New Zealand scenery as a backdrop. For me, it felt wonderful to have a link with the wider family after such a long time of its being just the four of us. It did mean, however, that I started the school year a week after the term had started – but my teacher was relaxed about that.

Within a short while of Uncle Bill's departure, plans started for the arrival of the next family members. My maternal grandparents had decided that they would immigrate to New Zealand once they retired. As time went on, there were discussions about this. The excitement began to build. My parents had plans drawn up to build on an extra bedroom and a bathroom for my grandparents. I remember Simon and me waving at any planes flying overhead.

On the final day of school in December 1976, there was a phone call to our home just as we were heading out the door. My mother took the call. I remember that she went pale and cried a little during the conversation. Afterwards, she was quiet as she bundled me and Simon off to school. I remember thinking that it was strange, but I got on with the events of the day.

After school, I was surprised to see my dad already home from work. Very quietly, my parents sat Simon and me down for a chat. I remember sitting together on the couch as Dad told us that Grandma had died in hospital in England. She had been unwell for a few days, but she had insisted that my mum not be told so that she would not worry from such a long distance.

I sat quietly beside my dad as we were told the news and just quietly cried. All four of us sat cuddled up and cried together. It seemed so cruel that she would die so close to the time that they would be moving out to New Zealand. I remember being too frightened to ask if Grandma was a friend of Jesus – in case the answer was no.

I desperately wanted to console my mum, but I was at a complete loss of what to say.

Gradually, over the next few days, more details came out and decisions were made. My grandfather decided that he would go ahead as planned and move to New Zealand in the following year. He asked my dad to return to England to help him pack up and make the trip, saying that he would reimburse my father's costs. We were not a wealthy family. At that time, air travel to the other side of the world was very expensive. It was not possible for my mum to return for my grandmother's funeral.

There was quite a shadow over the family and it was certainly a very quiet Christmas. One of the things that made it difficult was that Grandma had already posted Christmas cards and a Christmas parcel to us. It was extremely difficult for my mother as they arrived. They were very treasured gifts that year. I remember the Holly Hobbie doll that I was given. It was much loved and a source of comfort to me in the months ahead.

I grieved for my grandma very quietly. I had some wonderful memories, but even more than that I was sorry that I would now not have the opportunity to get to know her again. Naturally, it was an extremely tough time for my parents, particularly for my mother. In many ways, the world is a small place, but when there is a death in a family at such a distance, it feels like the world is enormous.

One day at the beginning of the holidays, Simon and I were playing in the garden on the swings that friends had given us. It was a set of two swings and they were particularly good. Instead of chains, they had metal bars which made it much easier to swing very high.

One particular day, we were having a competition to see who could jump off at the highest point. It was great fun. I got more and more adventurous and decided to go much higher. Simon pointed out that I was going too high. He even told me that he thought that I had won, but I was determined to push a bit higher.

My next jump was huge. It was followed by a double somersault and a loud crack as I landed on my right arm. I was beside myself. My brother went very pale and needless to say, my dad was very concerned. We made a trip to the hospital's emergency department. After some time, some toing and froing, and some X-rays, it was determined that my arm was fractured. Unfortunately, it was fractured just on the elbow joint, so I was not able to have it in plaster (which would have been cool, as I could have got everyone to sign the cast). My arm was bandaged instead. I had to have the bandage changed regularly so that the arm could be repositioned to prevent the elbow joint from becoming too stiff.

Initially, the fracture was painful, but the pain soon settled down. It was inconvenient to have a broken arm. I felt awkward with the large, cumbersome bandage on my right arm. It was hot and itchy underneath the bandage during a particularly hot Christchurch summer. I am right-handed, but I did quickly become very adept with my left arm.

That summer, I was to go on my first camp with the kids from church. I was very excited about going, but having a broken arm presented something of an obstacle. After much discussion, I was allowed to go to camp. The leaders took great care of me.

Camp was held at Living Springs, which is a beautiful Christian campsite in Governors Bay not far from Christchurch. Set on the hills, it has stunning views overlooking the harbour. It was not my first camp there, but it was my first kids' camp. I had a wonderful time.

In the afternoons at camp, we children were allowed to pick activities to try out. There was a variety of activities to choose from: horse riding, riding go-carts, making arts and crafts, dancing, and making a film. Well, having my arm in a bandage made some of the activities seem just too difficult. Still, the camp leaders were quick to encourage me and said that I could try anything I wanted to do. I decided to help with the making of a film, although I have no idea why that appealed to me. We decided to make a film about the parable of the prodigal son. It was lots of fun and they even put me in a shot – bandage and all – in the banquet scene at the end.

I was, all the while, learning that there was fun to be had while leading a Christian life. At camp and in children's church I was surrounded by grown-ups who took kids seriously. Even more important was that they took God seriously. They believed that God could do amazing things in the lives of children. They expected to see the Holy Spirit moving amongst us children. That certainly raised my expectation levels even further and I too expected to hear God talk to me and to see him work in my life.

I remember returning from camp and feeling ever so guilty. I had thoroughly enjoyed myself, but, on returning home, I felt badly for my mum, who was grieving for her mother. I felt frustrated - I so much wanted to say the right thing and make my mum feel better, but I had no idea at all what the right thing was.

At the end of the summer holidays, I returned to school for my final year in Primary School. For my Standard 4 year, there was a possibility of having two teachers, one a lady and one a man. Both were older and both were strict but, because the lady had been kind to me on a number of occasions, I hoped to be in her class. I was disappointed to discover that I had Mr Black, whom I perceived to be tough and grumpy. He was a middle-aged man who always smelt of cigarette smoke and was always gruff.

My arm came out of the bandages the week before I returned to school. I was ever so pleased to be free at last. However, six weeks of limited movement had left my arm a little stiff and somewhat weakened. It was a challenge being back at school. My arm was sore again, and I felt like I just couldn't keep up. Sunday night saw me in tears as I contemplated another week of school. Mum and Dad were so kind about it all and suggested that it might be a good idea to tell Mr Black so that he would understand that I was sore and struggling somewhat. That did seem like a good idea to me, but I was very afraid of Mr Black and couldn't face talking to him about my arm.

On the Monday morning, my mum came into school with me. She explained to Mr Black what I was struggling with. He made some reassuring comments and suggested that I could be his helper for a week or two during physical-education class rather than participate. Feeling better, I relaxed a little.

He then told me that I was a big girl now and that I should have told him that there was a problem rather than dragging Mum into school. He asked me if I thought he was scary. I said nothing, so he asked if I thought that he was going to eat me up and spit out my eyes as pips. I shook my head quietly, but I thought that maybe he might just do that.

My initial perceptions of Mr Black were to be confirmed. He ruled the class with a tough hand. He expected order and control. We became a much more serious class overnight.

Looking back, I see that Mr Black really was something of a bully. He would frequently remind us children that he had eyes in the back of his head. He had an uncanny ability to be writing on the blackboard and identifying that there was a disruption or some misbehaviour in the class. Without turning around, he would hit the culprit squarely on the body with the chalk that he had just been writing with. He would then not say a word but would stand with his hand out, waiting for the petrified child to return the piece of chalk. I knew that he could not possibly have eyes in the back of his head, but there were certainly times when his unnerving accuracy made me wonder.

As the year went by, Mr Black's behaviour towards the class became less stringent, but his behaviour towards me became more inappropriate. Gradually, he became more intrusive of my personal space. He would place me in the classroom in a corner and then draw close to me. He isolated me from my friends in the class. I was never seated beside them and was always placed in different work groups. Initially he would stand too close. Later, he would place his hand on my shoulder and then on my thigh or on my bottom. I disliked him immensely. His touch was revolting to me.

Mr Black was intimidating, and he seemed to enjoy intimidating me. He knew that I was frightened of him, and it was clear that my fear pleased him.

I tried to disappear. I became quieter and I behaved impeccably to avoid his attention. I worked hard to finish my work quickly and well, doing anything to ensure that he would not focus on me.

He started to play mind games. He would mark my work as wrong when it was right. He would give me copious amounts of make-up work to do. He would do things like write words into my spelling book, spelling them wrong. I remember that he wrote "diffarant" into my spelling book. If I used the word and spelt it the way it was in my spelling book, then he would smile. If I chose to spell it right, then he would mark it wrong, humiliate me in front of the class, and send me away to practise writing it the "right" way.

One day, our class had a relieving teacher. She pulled me up for my spelling of *different*. She asked me to bring my spelling book up to her. Surprised to see how the word was written in my book, she rewrote it, spelling it correctly. She gave me a strange look and then signed her name beside the place where she had respelt the word.

When Mr Black returned to school and saw my spelling book, he was furious and threw stuff off his desk in great anger. I was left with the great dilemma of how to spell *different*. After due consideration, I wrote it correctly. After that, Mr Black said nothing else about it.

Mr Black hated church and Christians. I remember once that he told us children about his experience with going to Sunday school. He described the room to us and explained that in the centre of the room there was a pot-belly stove that always had a fire lit in it. The teacher would have a kettle on the stove to heat water to make a cup of tea. One day, she had knocked the kettle over. The hot water went everywhere, including over him. He explained that this meant that Christians could not be trusted and that they were mean. He made jibes about Christians all school year.

Mr Black also talked about his daughter who was off to the Antarctica as part of a research team. He was very proud of her, but he added the comment that none of us students were as clever as she was. He told us that we were not likely to amount to much.

Things came to a head one day. It was a lovely, warm day, a break from the recent appalling weather, so the class was finally able to have some outside play. I was not permitted to join them, however. Towards the end of the morning, Mr Black complained bitterly about the standard of my work. He told me that I would have to remain inside to complete it properly at lunchtime.

I was gutted, because I had looked forward to having some playtime with my friends. I was angry because I knew that there was nothing wrong with the standard of the work. I was frightened because I was terrified of this man. I was afraid to the point of wanting to be sick.

When the lunch bell went off, the rest of the class filed out to wash their hands and go out to eat their lunch. I sat down at my desk to start the work over again. Mr Black came back into the room and told me to put my things away. He said that nothing was wrong with my work – that it was, in fact, good work – but that he just wanted some time with me. Very afraid, I started to cry. He told me to come and to say thank you to him. I stood up but then I looked at him and I couldn't move. He told me again to come to him. Again, I seemed to be frozen to the spot.

In an instant, he had me held down on the floor. I continued to cry. His hands undid my clothing. I was scared and stunned and just kept saying no over and over again. It seemed to go on forever. I had turned my head to look away. When I looked back, I saw that he had his shorts undone and had himself fully exposed. I was crying and saying no, but he was very angry and determined. What he did to me in those moments on that day was invasive, unlawful, and degrading. For a long time, I could still feel the touch of his hands and the smell of his body.

There was a noise from in the cloakroom. He was frustrated at being interrupted and angry but I was released and very quickly I fixed my clothes and then ran outside. I hid under some trees at the back of the school playground and prayed that lunchtime would never end.

What happened that day was something that Mr Black never attempted again. In many ways, his behaviour towards me changed from that day on. There was coldness in how he interacted with me. He remained very intrusive of my personal space, usually when he wanted to be intimidating for some reason. He would touch me. Unconsciously, my body would shrink away from him and try to shrug off his hand. He would laugh and hold onto me all the firmer.

Sometimes he would come close to me and murmur little comments to me. Things said to intimidate and frighten but mostly, I can now see they were said to keep me quiet. He would say things like the following: "Your parents know what happened, and they think that it was OK"; "Nobody would believe you if you said anything"; "Nobody would really care about it"; "You should be grateful that someone paid you any attention"; "God doesn't really care or else he would have stopped me"; "Nobody will ever love you or want you"; "What man will want you now?"; and "It wasn't really wrong." Only once he told me, "It is your fault because you brought it upon yourself."

They were all words that became like grooves in a record that I would repeat over and over again to myself in the years ahead. It was like I was programmed to think in a certain way about things. With hindsight, I can see with great clarity that Mr Black's campaign was about keeping me quiet and protecting his own neck.

He was always a bully, both with me and with the other girls in the class. Actually, he was a bully with everyone – even other teaching staff. The classroom enjoyed a sense of pleasant relief when he was off sick for a few weeks and we had relieving staff. All in all, it was a very long year.

There were other things happening that year. My dad went to the United Kingdom to return with my mother's stepfather. Dad was away for only a short time, but it seemed like forever. Mum was not herself. Even when Dad did return, things were different. Granddad didn't really make a concerted effort to settle in. He was moody and withdrawn, he was difficult to please and was very critical of Simon and me.

For the time that our grandfather stayed with us, Simon and I shared a bedroom in order to accommodate him. I felt embattled at home and school. The days were terrifying, and the nights were no reprieve, as I battled nightmares and often awoke in a hot sweat. I craved my own space.

Granddad stayed for only a few months before deciding to return to the United Kingdom.

All in all it was an unsettled year. With so much turbulence around, any changes in me or in my behaviour went unnoticed. I told no one what had happened to me and I buried the memories away. I didn't brood on things or try to make any sense of it all. I just buried all the memories and pretended that what Mr Black did had never happened.

Late that year, Granddad returned to England. He inflicted some pain on his exit. He was unwise in some of what he said and unfortunately some of the items that he had given us as gifts, he now requested back. It must have been a very difficult time for my parents, but they stood strong and helped us all through it. I remember being so very impressed by my mother's dignity in the situation. She truly behaved with great honour. Much as I was sad to see Granddad leave, I was particularly sad to see my radio leave with him! It was good to have my bedroom back and my family back. However, another of my family's links to the United Kingdom was broken.

Change of Schools

The next year saw a change of schools for me which was a little overwhelming but an amazing opportunity. I started at Middleton Grange School in Form 1 (Year 7). It was a wonderful Christian school that proved to be an amazing safe haven for me. I felt very safe. I could relax.

I made great friends with the girls in my class, and I thrived in the environment. Academically, I held my own. Even more special was the opportunity to learn much more about God and to continue to develop my relationship with him.

There were drawbacks to Middleton Grange School. It was very far from home, necessitating a lot of travel to and from school. The cost of the school fees meant that sending me there was a sacrificial choice made by my parents.

It also meant that any changes in my behaviour were explained away by the change of school and then the onset of puberty. I think that, at this point, I could not have explained what Mr Black had done to me. I'm not sure that I could categorise it in any way. His programming was working well. I repeated his messages to myself regularly. I convinced myself that whatever had happened was my fault and that I had probably brought it all upon myself. I started not trusting people, particularly men. I avoided being alone with men, except for my dad. I remain very grateful that I had a great relationship with my father.

Even through all of this, God was very gracious and continued to bless me with a special relationship with him. He blessed me with amazing friends and amazing mentors who loved me.

During this time I remember having a conversation with my mum. I was lying on the floor in the lounge. She was on the floor beside me reading the newspaper when she looked up and told me that Mr Black was being sent to prison for how he had treated a girl in his class at school. My heart was racing and I wondered if she was going to ask me if anything like that had happened when he taught me. I managed to say, "Oh, right." Later, Mum said that I didn't seem surprised to hear the news.

At the time, I did not volunteer any information. I had convinced myself that nothing had really happened and that I had imagined it. Yet here I was confronted with the news that Mr Black was going to prison. It seemed that the girl concerned was a year behind me in school. His treatment of her was uncovered. In later years, I wondered whether he groomed someone each year to abuse. He was certainly very skilled in his psychological manipulations of me.

The article in the paper said that Mr Black had pleaded not guilty. At that moment, I knew that it would always be his word against mine if I said anything. He had told me that no one would believe me, and I believed him.

After two years at Middleton Grange, I changed schools yet again. The fees at Middleton Grange were high, and travelling to school was taking its toll. For me, moving this time was a wrench made harder by the fact that I was now old enough to understand the reasons why.

My experience at Koinonia Christian School was poles apart from my experience at Middleton Grange School. I found it exceedingly difficult to make friends at my new school. Most of the other kids attended the same church or had been at the school a lot longer than I, so they all knew each other very well. I was quiet and seen as a goody two shoes. I guess that in many ways I was. I had learnt to behave as well as possible in order to avoid any unwanted attention. At Middleton Grange, I had learnt that behaving myself would earn me some very pleasant positive reinforcement.

I do remember a teacher at Koinonia telling me that things would be easier for me if I wasn't so good all the time. A ridiculous statement, really!

On top of my difficulty at school, adolescence was not kind to me. I was bothered by acne and I had become very curvy. I thought that I was terribly fat when, in fact, the changes were simply my feminine curves arriving. But I was insecure and I hated my body very much. I felt that it had betrayed me and had made me vulnerable to Mr Black.

All in all, I hated Koinonia Christian School. I was bullied and teased about how I looked and how I behaved. Those were two tough years. I felt incredibly isolated and alone. I began to spend long periods of time on my own in my bedroom. I read copious amounts and spent a lot of time in an imaginary world. Escape, while blissful, was always short-lived.

When it came to academics, this school was a much poorer choice. My parents and I would later discover that I had developed some significant gaps in my learning.

Things were difficult at home during this time as well. Two teenagers in a home and all of life's usual bumps can make life difficult. It is easy to be aware of the things that you are facing as an individual, but multiply that by the number of people in the home and things become intense, to say the least. Even so, I was aware of things that the others in my family were dealing with. Understanding how much was landing on my mum's plate, I resolved that I would not add to it. Any difficulties were kept in house and were not discussed with anyone else. I think that to people outside the family, things were just carrying on as normal.

One year with that man had changed me in many ways. I felt estranged and distant from family and others to whom I might have turned. The incredible mind games that Mr Black played with me left me convinced that no one would ever believe what I might say about his behaviour. I became the compliant teenager who learned to behave and simply fly under the radar.

My own headspace was unravelling as I was increasingly unhappy about my life. I felt like my life was full of secrets. There seemed to be many things that I had to internalise and couldn't share.

Schoolwork was a struggle for me. I passed the work, but I had to make a considerable effort to do so. Nipping at my heels was a younger brother who seemed to fly through school with little effort. He was clever, sociable, athletic, and charming. It seemed to me that he was the very opposite of me. I felt as if my life was a disaster. I felt like I was living in Simon's shadow. Curiously, however, this didn't cause me to resent him.

Church remained an anchor for me. In some ways, it was similar to other parts of my life. At church, I had few friends and was teased for being good. I was estranged from many of my peers, but there were those amongst the leaders who took an interest in me and were very kind to me. I think that they were oblivious to my internal angst or, at least, to the extent that I was struggling. I did find that I could lose myself in the presence of God. I had an amazing appetite to learn as much as I possibly could about God. During those years, I found that my best friend was God. God, in his great mercy, talked to me often.

My teen years were not at all easy. I lunged from one difficulty to another. My body changed, and the process was painful and unpleasant. I found it increasingly difficult to make friends. I had a handful of friends, but I found it hard to open up with them and to share anything that was in any way intimate. I found people hard to trust. Also, I lived with a great fear of being discovered. I trusted no one. More than anything, I shied away from boys and men. I thought that I was a bad person. I was frightened that people would know what had happened to me just by spending time with me.

I had another change of schools and went from Koinonia Christian School to the local state school, Avonside Girls' High School. It was a shock going from a school of twenty high-school students to one with eight hundred girls. I also found it overwhelming to go from a very controlled environment to somewhere that was much looser. I experienced significant culture shock.

I was also stunned to find that I had gone from being an above-average student at Middleton Grange to being seriously at risk of failing. I was, however, self-disciplined and determined. I knuckled down and put my very best into the work. I worked hard and managed to get my marks up to a level where I passed, but with not a lot of room to spare.

I made friends at school, but I remained a very private person who preferred time to herself. The girls were, by and large, kind to me. I was not teased. Although not popular, I found that things were much improved. I lacked confidence, which was not at all helped by my struggling with the schoolwork. The teaching staff were very supportive and looked out for me. For me, my time at Avonside was a great school experience.

As time went on, I found that church was a mixed bag for me. I felt on the outside in terms of friends amongst my peers at church. Looking back, I think that I just didn't fit the mould. Then again, my lagging confidence ensured that I didn't try to fit in. I remained on the outer, hating my social position. I found myself feeling jealous of the other girls with their pretty faces, trendy clothes, and masses of friends. I craved intimacy in friendship, but I dreaded it completely. I was very frightened that someone would discover my secret. I felt so dirty.

On the other hand, I began to find a place for myself in the church community. My parents were leading a house group and, therefore, we had masses of people through the house. They were an interesting mix of people. Many of them were also on the outer. I guess that many of them would have been considered to be odd bods, but I thought they were a great bunch of people. I learnt about God's family and about loving the unlovable. I learnt the power of unconditional love – that people can change just by knowing that they are loved and accepted. That in fact, you can overlook a lot of personality quirks with a great big dose of love and acceptance. I also learnt the value of good hospitality. I watched my mother be a hostess and work to make other people comfortable.

What Will I Do When I Am Grown Up?

I started to teach Sunday school. I enjoyed it and loved the time with the children. I particularly enjoyed watching them open up to God and seeing the wonder in their faces as they came face-to-face with him. I decided that I wanted to teach, to be a primary school teacher. I became focused on that as my goal and really would not consider anything else.

Uncle Bill visited again for a week which we all felt was not long enough, although we understood the limitations of annual leave. It was wonderful to see him again. Impressed with my ability to drive him to church, he resolved to learn to drive upon his return to the United Kingdom.

In my final year of school, I applied to go teaching but I was disappointed to be wait-listed for a place. It really hadn't occurred to me that I would not get into Teachers College and I certainly had no back-up plan. I was gutted – made worse when a couple of school friends were offered admission to the college.

What to do? I knew that I did not want to go to university. It seemed to me that to go to university would be to fill in time until I knew what I could do or wanted to do. To my very practical mind, doing that seemed to be a waste of time, energy, and money. Many of my former classmates were headed that way and it was just assumed that I too would go. The school's careers advisor suggested that I look into nursing, but I would not even consider it.

I scrambled for other options and, in the meantime, applied for every job that I thought might be a possibility. I was turned down for some of these on the basis that the interviewers thought I was too bright and that I would be bored too quickly. This was complicated by the fact that I was young to be finishing school and, therefore, did not meet the criteria for some training options.

There was some pressure from my parents who made it clear that I would need to do something. For me to sit at home doing nothing was not an option. I decided that I would look for some work in an office. My mother suggested that Polytechnic might have some classes that would give me a taste of that kind of work and help me to develop some of the necessary skills.

After I graduated from high school, my parents very generously offered me the opportunity to spend the summer holiday with my mother's aunt in Sydney. It was a wonderful chance to see something of Australia and to meet more of the extended family.

I took the opportunity. This meant that I spent my first Christmas away from family. But I was well fussed over and thoroughly spoilt at my mother's aunt's home. Christmas was a hot day, even for Sydney, with a temperature of 36°C at 9 a.m. and continuing to rise. Uncle Rob dressed in full Santa attire to deliver the presents to the younger grandchildren. Christmas dinner was a full traditional Christmas dinner with all the trimmings – in spite of the heat.

The New Year started with my beginning to study business and office systems at Polytechnic. I made some good friends, but I was quickly bored. Many of my classmates were feeling challenged, but I certainly was not.

I had a reprieve mid-year when I was offered a job. I had applied for something with this firm early in the year, but I had been turned down after being shortlisted. Now they wanted to offer me a position as an office Junior.

The position was in the Christchurch office of a large international accountancy firm. It was very much a junior position and was not well paid. However, it was an alternative to being very bored sitting in my class at Polytechnic. After discussing it with my parents, I accepted the job, but with the understanding that I would continue some of my classes at night school.

The office was located in a ten-storey building overlooking Cathedral Square right in the centre of the central business district of Christchurch. The staff were kind enough. I settled into the routine. It was an interesting environment, with quite a differentiation between partners, the accounting staff, and the administrative staff. I really was the lowest of the low. The young woman whom I had replaced was still employed there but had been promoted within the ranks. She was to induct me into my position.

Initially, all was well at work. I was stimulated by learning the job and finding my own ways of doing things. After six months, however, I was unhappy.

It didn't matter how hard I worked. I never got on top of everything. There was always a list of things to do. Mind, I did find that I was being given increasing amounts of work to do by my predecessor on top of mine – but very quietly. It came as a surprise to my manager later on to see how much of her work was actually being completed by me. I felt on the outer. I also felt looked down upon.

Before long, I was bored, as the job was tedious. There was an occasional glimmer of hope when I was asked to help with specific projects that were outside my usual job description. These provided stimulus, and I excelled at them. It was great to exercise my brain.

However, by the time that I had been in the job for a year, I was absolutely miserable. My mood was low and my self-confidence was even lower. Things came to a crunch one day. I knew that I needed to make a move in some direction. Things would have to change.

I decided that I would apply for further training. I was still interested in teaching, so I decided that I would apply again, but this time in both Christchurch and Sydney. I gave some thought to nursing. After doing further research, I decided to apply – again, in Christchurch and Sydney. Applications were sent and prayers were offered.

By the time the application closure dates had arrived, my heart and mind had shifted to a preference to nursing.

One by one I heard back. I was on the wait list for a place at Teacher's College in Christchurch. I was offered a nursing training place in Sydney. Then I was offered a teaching training position in Sydney. The next one was nursing in Christchurch. I remember arriving home to find a letter for me on the table. My experience was that thin letters contained a no answer and thick envelopes contained a yes answer. This letter was small and thin. My heart sank. My mind raced at a great pace as I contemplated a move to Sydney.

I opened the letter to find an invitation to an information morning complete with an interview time. I was stunned. Quickly, I replied that I would be in attendance. I braced myself to ask for a morning off at work.

I assumed that the future was still up in the air, although later I learned that I had already been shortlisted for a place.

The information session was wonderful. The more I heard about the training, the more excited I was about the possibilities it held for me.

My only hesitation was that I would become a poor student again. My parents, however, were encouraging and supportive.

Finally a thick envelope arrived. The letter inside invited me to enrol to study nursing at Christchurch Polytechnic. Without hesitating, I accepted the offer. I enrolled for the following year, to start at the beginning of February. I wrote to the places in Sydney to decline their offers.

Ironically, a week later I was offered a position at Teacher's College, Christchurch. Again, there was no hesitation. I knew without any doubt which was the right door to go through. I couldn't wait to begin.

At the point when I had decided that I needed a change in direction, I also thought that I needed a goal or something to look forward to. Gradually, I decided that I would save up and travel to England for a holiday.

I saved hard, researched intently, and applied for extended leave, as using all of my annual leave would not be quite enough. My trip, booked for November onwards, was booked long before I knew that I was going to start nursing in the following year.

Suddenly, things were improving. I had felt lost and aimless. I was stuck in a giant rut and was becoming increasingly frustrated. Now I found myself with a holiday to look forward to. Beyond that, a whole new chapter was going to open up.

As my holiday approached, I started to worry about my fees and costs for Polytechnic. I had managed to do really well with my saving, but now I began to wonder if it would be wiser to keep my money for course costs. I was, however, committed to taking a trip to England, which, in hindsight, turned out to be a very good thing.

My trip took me away for about eight weeks. I was to spend a month in London, staying with my uncle Bill, and then I would be based with my aunt and her family near Manchester. The thought was that I would spend Christmas with Uncle Bill and then New Year with my cousins. My flight to the United Kingdom took me via Singapore, where I had an overnight stay, and then on to London.

Uncle Bill met me at Heathrow Airport mid morning and took me home. He had very kindly arranged to have a couple of days off work in order to show me around a little. I remember being very tired, but he insisted that I should stay awake until the evening, as this would help adjust my body clock.

That first day, Uncle Bill and a friend of his took me to Canterbury for the day. I remember falling in love with the old cathedral and the narrow streets.

The following day, he took me into the city of London on the train and taught me how to get around London on the trains and the Underground. The Underground was very big, very busy, and very noisy. I loved it! Uncle Bill wisely recommended that I avoid travelling at peak hour.

For the next few weeks, Uncle Bill and I fell into a very easy pattern. He continued to work. I would head out sightseeing or shopping, and then I would return to his place and start to get an evening meal ready. I managed to see so much and hopefully did not inconvenience him too much. My stay at his house was very relaxed. It helped that I already knew him well.

While in England, I attended Church of England services, first with Uncle Bill and later by myself. It certainly was a very different form of worship. I found it thought-provoking.

My plans altered a little when my aunt insisted that I spend Christmas with her and her family. A couple of days before I had initially planned to, I travelled to her home by bus from London to Manchester.

I had not seen my aunt, uncle, cousins, or grandparents since I was three years old. It felt exceedingly awkward to be with them. I think that I was not at all what they were expecting. It did feel to me that they were a little disappointed. I was unwell with a cold during the middle of my stay. I remember feeling ill, lonely, and incredibly homesick.

The trip home, already a long one, was made longer when the flight was delayed for ten hours at Manchester Airport because of fog. This included a wait of three hours in the plane on the tarmac while the crew tried to locate a truck that had gone missing between London and Manchester. The truck was carrying luggage for the flight.

It was good to be home and I returned to work to finish my last few weeks. I had managed to have a truly amazing holiday, to see so much and to come home with a little money left in my pocket! The remaining money was just the right amount that I would need to spend on textbooks!

Going to work was easy when I knew that I was finishing. I had been back at work a few days when I was asked to see one of the partners. I must confess that I was afraid that he was going to growl at me, although I didn't know what he had to growl about.

It turned out that when the company had paid me my holiday pay, they overpaid me by a few hundred dollars. My heart sank as I contemplated having to repay the amount. The partner explained that it was their mistake (which is embarrassing for a firm full of accountants) and that the law allowed them to deduct a small amount from each of my pay cheques to recover the overpayment.

After explaining this, the partner smiled, winked at me, and said that instead of having me repay the money, the company would like me to consider it to be a donation towards my course costs. I started to breathe again.

An Eye to the Medal

Starting at Polytechnic was like experiencing the first day of school all over again. It was a beautiful, sunny day. All of us students assembled together outside as a large group before being separated off into individual classes. There were ten classes of fifteen students. I eyed up my class of fifteen and wondered what their stories were and what they were like as individuals. I had prayed for some good friends and had asked God for another Christian in the group. Looking around the group, I wondered if my prayer would be answered.

Our first task was to introduce ourselves to the others in the group and gradually we began to relax. There was quite a range of people in terms of age and backgrounds. It proved to be an interesting mix. Over the three years, my group gained the reputation of being a class that was a formidable team working together. By and large, we got along very well and looked out for each other.

I very quickly got into the momentum of studying. Although I had never been much of a student, this time was different. I was passionate about nursing, and I was determined to do well. It seemed to me that when I was finally a nurse, my future patients would expect me to know as much as possible. I studied long and hard and soon gained a reputation of being a studious goody-good.

The first year at Polytechnic was to be almost entirely theory work, with a mix of clinical and theory to follow in the second and third years. The mix of subjects was interesting and stimulating – biology, chemistry, microbiology, physics, psychology, sociology, and communication. I soon gained favourites, but I applied myself to everything.

Classes at the School of Nursing at Christchurch Polytechnic at this stage were, by and large, held in small, prefabricated classrooms that were linked by walkways largely covered by pergolas. The set-up worked well, although on cold windy winter days there was no loitering during room changes. On the other hand there were plenty of grassed courtyards to enjoy during lunch breaks. As we graduated three years later, the school had a new multilevel building opened to house nursing students as well as those studying other sciences.

Things progressed well over the first year. I made some friends in my class, in particular Romy (who was also a Christian – an answer to my prayer) and Robynne. I passed my tests and assignments with flying colours.

It has to be said that I put myself under extraordinary pressure at Polytechnic. Over time, that stress began to show. At this point, it showed up in subtle ways. I was sleeping less well and I was very anxious at times. At the time, I put this down to my workload at Polytechnic, as the other students were complaining about the workload and the expectations. With hindsight it is clear that my perfectionist tendency ensured that I was absolutely driven. I was beginning to lose perspective on things.

Another change this year was that I changed churches. I had felt disconnected from my peers at the New Life Centre for some time, so I started attending services at St Stephen's Anglican Church. I enjoyed the family nature of the congregation. There were not many people in my age group, but the small group of us became friends. A study group was formed around us. Interestingly, although there were not many of us, as I looked around the rest of the group I became very aware of how very clever they all were. The study group provided the setting for some very interesting and intense discussions. From my very Pentecostal upbringing, I found the Anglican liturgy to be grounding and strangely reassuring.

As the New Year swung into action, we nursing students were very excited (and a little apprehensive) about starting Year 2. Clinical placements meant that we were required to master a whole new range of skills. We relished it even though some of the skills were unpleasant, especially given that we were practising them on each other.

I will always remember having to give Romy an injection and, on another day, inserting a nasogastric tube into her. Mind, it wasn't very pleasant having her do the same to me.

There were fun moments too. We had been taught the very practical skill of making hospital beds, complete with hospital corners. At the end of one morning, there was a race off to see who could make a bed the fastest. Bear in mind that the standard still had to be high. I am pleased to say that Romy and I did not disgrace ourselves.

I must admit that during the holidays prior to Year 2, my mum had spent some time teaching me some of the basics so that I didn't show her up. Tips in things like taking temperatures, positioning patients in their bed and bed making. Mostly she talked to me about how things really were on the wards – the staff dynamics and workloads. What I learnt from her certainly helped my confidence no end.

For some nursing students, actually hitting the wards comes as a shock. Some find themselves reconsidering their suitability for nursing. As for me, I loved working on the wards. I threw myself into the task, boots and all. The way rotation was set for my class in our second year meant that most of our placements were hospital-based:

medical, surgical, paediatrics, and orthopaedics. The third year would include endocrinology, psychiatry, and obstetrics.

I pushed myself to learn as much as I could. I was conscientious. I discovered that I worked well in a team. Consequently, staff took well to me. This meant that I was offered extra opportunities to observe or assist with all manner of procedures. With the exception of one placement, I was taken aside by charge nurses who expressed their positive assessment of my clinical placement and my ever increasing skills. They then recommended that I apply for a job in their department at the end of my rotation!

I was often blessed with being in the right place at the right time, or maybe it is more appropriate to say that I was in an interesting place at the right time.

By the time I finished my Year 2 clinical placements, I had been present for two cases of cardiac arrest, a case of anaphylactic shock, and a case of a ruptured aortic aneurysm. I learnt that I kept a cool head in emergencies and that my instincts were good.

Life had been reasonably smooth for me through my first and second years of training. It is true to say that while many of my fellow students were encouraged to focus and study hard, I was encouraged to relax more and to take time out. I remember one tutor allocating homework and starting with, "For you all, except Suzanne, homework for tonight is…. Suzanne, you should watch TV or read a novel." I did the homework that was set for the rest of the class, as the teacher knew I would!

By my third year, things were starting to seriously unravel. Any perfectionistic tendencies that I might have shown earlier now accelerated into some very obsessive tendencies. I went beyond being self-disciplined to being completely controlling of myself.

I became controlling in my eating habits. My diet became more healthy, but then I moved beyond that to become extremely restrictive. I ate smaller amounts. Although I cut out some unhealthy items from my diet, I also cut out vital components, including protein and carbohydrates. I was sneaky with it, though, implying to others that I had already eaten. I was frequently hungry, but I would never have admitted that.

I became feverish about exercising for the first time in my life. Not surprisingly, I lost weight. Unsurprisingly, this was noted by friends, fellow students, and tutors. I was dismissive of their concerns. Most people put my weight loss down to the stress of study and my workload.

Fun disappeared from my life. To a large extent, my life was nursing and sleep. I was either in class, in the wards or studying. I was performing well - my ward reports were excellent and my assessment marks/grades were brilliant but I was terrified of failing.

I had friends, good friends, but increasingly I was withdrawn. I also felt like I was living behind a façade. My self-esteem was at an all-time low.

About a third of the way through my third year of study, things deteriorated markedly following a class for one of our psychiatric units.

We students were in class for a couple of weeks studying theory related to a number of areas, including alcoholism and substance abuse. Amongst these were some sessions on the abuse cycle. We had previously studied the abuse cycle, but this time it was more of a look at *why* people abuse others.

I sat in class feeling increasingly uncomfortable. Somewhat agitated, I felt sick in the pit of my stomach. The lecture was supplemented by a video which included interviews with a number of men who had abused others. In their own words, they explored what had happened and why they had done it. I listened to their horrendous stories about domestic violence and other abuses. Five minutes into the documentary, I stood to leave the room. As I left the room, I muttered, "That is rubbish." For the first time in my life, I slammed the door behind me. My only thought was to get out of the room. I remember having no idea what to do next. It was very cold outside, but I didn't care. Initially, I appreciated the cold air.

Romy followed me out of the class to check that I was alright. I remember saying that I was just very angry about what the men were saying. They were justifying their appalling behaviour. There was no excuse for what they did. I was so angry and so upset, but I was careful to give Romy no hint of my story or history. I do remember the quizzical look that Romy gave me.

I did not return to class for the rest of the session. No one said anything about my disappearance – at least not to me.

That day changed everything. I knew why I had reacted the way that I had. I also knew that if I was not exceptionally careful, the rather large secret would be out and I would be completely exposed. I thought that if I was just self-disciplined and watched my step, then all would be well.

But another hurdle was introduced that day. I started having nightmares or rather what would come to be a recurring nightmare. In my sleep, my mind would return me to that classroom where I had been on the receiving end of Mr Black's abuse many years earlier. It was like a film replaying in my mind in the darkest hours of the night. The nightmare arrived that first night and then returned regularly afterwards. There were nights when I did not have the nightmare, but then it would soon return. By day, I was driven and a perfectionist in my work and study. At night, I returned to my bed in fear of where my dreams would take me that night.

Somehow I was managing to function most of the time, but increasingly people were becoming concerned about me.

A Brief Return to the Past

I remember one of my nursing tutors pulling me aside at the end of a class for a chat about how things were going. I admitted feeling tired and a little stressed, but nothing more. She was ever so kind and reassured me that a number of students struggled with stress in their final year.

With hindsight, I wonder whether my tutor suspected there was more going on. If she did, she didn't indicate it to me. She did, however, suggest that there would be benefit in arranging a time to talk to the counsellor based at the Polytechnic Health Centre. She suggested that the staff at the health centre were particularly helpful in teaching time-management skills and relaxation skills. It sounded OK, but I was not convinced.

At this point, Romy stepped in and pointed out that I had nothing to lose and that seeing a counsellor might even be helpful. I agreed to go, but just once.

An appointment was made. I diligently turned up at the appointed time.

I was nervous and very unsure about what to expect. Rosemary, my counsellor, was a lovely, gentle lady who was kind and who tried hard to be reassuring. We talked at length about my workload and my study habits. She suggested a few things for me to try and asked me to return the next week. I was not at all sure that this was a good idea.

I made a concerted effort to try some of the things that Rosemary had suggested, but they made little difference. I knew the reason for that! I knew that I had not given my counsellor all of the information that she really needed to help me.

For a few weeks, I returned to see Rosemary even though I saw no real change in my life. I remained tired, stressed, and obsessive in my routines.

One day, I returned to see her with the objective of telling her that it would be my last time. She was friendly as ever and asked how my week had been. We chatted for a few moments. Then, to my surprise, she suddenly leant forward in her chair (which now made her very close) and looked me straight in the eye. She spoke very quietly.

She told me that she was concerned about me, that I seemed to be doing what she asked of me but that I seemed to continue to be rather stressed. She looked me in the eye and asked if there was something else that I needed to tell her. I was absolutely stunned and speechless.

Then I cried.

Trembling, I sat with tears rolling down my face. I doubt that I could have spoken, and I made no attempt to.

Rosemary was gentle and very kind. She took my hand and said that I needed time to think. She suggested that I return the next week, when we could talk. I nodded my agreement and then left.

Oh, I was such a mess as I stumbled back to classes. Poor Romy was concerned, but I was not going to explain what was going on – not yet, anyway.

It took a couple of days before I was able to explain to Romy that I was making no real progress and that Rosemary had reached the conclusion that there was something else I needed to tell her. Romy looked me straight in the eye and asked, "Is there? Tell me the truth." I swallowed and said that I thought there might be something. The room grew very quiet for a few moments before Romy replied, "Well, you should tell her then."

It was a long week, one during which I rode a roller-coaster ride. I was desperate to cancel my appointment, but I knew that if I walked in to cancel, I risked bumping into Rosemary.

On the day before my appointment, I was sure that I wouldn't go. Around lunchtime, Romy looked at me and said, "You're thinking of not going tomorrow, aren't you?" I laughed. I mean, what could I say? I explained that I didn't want to go to my appointment because I just didn't know how to say what I had to say. Romy's solution was that I write it down.

That evening, I gathered pen and paper and wrote down my dream. I thought that it might be the key.

The next morning, I arrived to see Rosemary. I was three minutes late. Usually, I was never late. This time I was late because I really did not want to be there. I had wrestled all night. Rosemary was usually in her office, and someone in reception would normally let her know that I was there. This time, she was waiting at reception. Nothing was said about it, but she knew very well that I had battled to be there.

We went through to her office and took our seats. There were no pleasantries exchanged this morning. Very quietly, she said, "Suzanne, you look very tired. You look unhappy about being here. Is there something we should talk about?"

My heart was racing. The room was filled with the noise of the clock ticking.

I shook my head.

"So why are you here?"

I heard more ticking of the clock, and yet time seemed to be standing still.

My hands were sweating, my heart was racing, and I suddenly felt very sick.

Quietly, I reached into my bag and pulled out the piece of paper, which I then handed to Rosemary. She showed reluctance to take hold of it, but she did accept it from me. Without reading it, she asked, "What do you want to talk about?" Again silence. "Suzanne …"

"I don't want to talk about it. I don't want to talk about anything. I have written down a dream that I keep having. I don't want to talk about anything."

Rosemary then read all that I had written down. She looked up at me. I prayed for the floor to open up and swallow me. It didn't.

"Suzanne, how long have you been having this dream?"

"A few months."

"Suzanne, how often do you have this dream?"

"A few nights a week. Sometimes more than once in a night."

"Suzanne, we need to talk about this dream, don't we?"

"No."

"Suzanne?"

"No."

"I think we do."

"No."

As the clock ticked, tears began to fall down my face. I bent down and picked up my bag to go. As I straightened up, Rosemary said, "Suzanne, I just want to ask one question – Suzanne!" I looked her straight in the eye. "Suzanne, is this a dream or a memory?"

I forced a smile on my face. "Yes."

"Yes?"

"It is a dream and it is a memory. I do not want to talk about it. I want to go now."

"Will you come and see me next week?"

"I do not want to talk about this."

"Will you come and see me, please?"

"But …"

"Suzanne, I need to check in with you. Please!"

"OK, but I need to go now."

The rest of the day was a blur. I was emotionally exhausted, and I desperately wanted some time alone. This was the first time I had acknowledged what had happened to me. I felt sick, and I was scared. Romy wanted to know what had happened with Rosemary.

She asked if I had talked about things. She wanted to know more, but I was most certainly not up for talking. I said enough to reassure her, but little more.

It was a long week of going through the motions and forcing a smile to appear on my face. It was a long week. A week of avoiding things. I did not want to think about things, about what I'd said, about what Rosemary had said, and certainly not about what might happen next. I threw myself into study and into a punishing exercise regime. I wanted to avoid thinking. I refused to even think about whether or not I would go to my counselling session the following week.

I still don't know why I went back to see Rosemary, but I did go. I must, however, confess that I was belligerent and difficult during my visit. I was in a resistive mood on arrival, but Rosemary was well ready for me.

The seating was different this week. A box of tissues was strategically placed near my chair. My heart sank. It was very hard for me to be grumpy and rude to someone when it was clear that she really did care and that she wanted to help me.

Rosemary stopped me in my tracks. "So, how are you, Suzanne?"

"OK."

"Really?"

"No, but …"

"I'm glad you came."

"I wasn't sure I would."

"I know. Suzanne, we do need to talk about it."

"No!"

"Suzanne, I understand that this is difficult, but you need to talk about it. I think that this is the time to start to talk."

"No."

"Let's do it this way. I will ask you some questions and you can go when you need to. OK?"

"No ... OK."

"Suzanne, have you ever told anyone else?"

"No."

"You really were very brave."

"No, no, I wasn't brave at all."

"Yes, you were brave to tell."

"No. I would say that I was desperate and falling apart."

"I can understand that you think you are falling apart, but you aren't."

Over the next half hour, there was further general discussion. I revealed no new information. To her credit, she did not push for any more. She needed to know that I was hanging in there, and she needed to convey to me that she cared. Even with her gentle approach, I suddenly felt the need to go. The session was all so very tiring and confronting.

Over the next few months I saw Rosemary on a weekly or fortnightly basis as our schedules allowed. She pushed me gently to change my perspectives on matters and to acknowledge more fully what had happened. I was reluctant and therefore often resistive.

Under New Zealand's Accident Compensation laws, I, as a victim of sexual abuse, was entitled to compensation and assistance. I had a very vague awareness of that. One day, Rosemary raised it as an issue with me. The rules were changing, which meant that what I was entitled to would also change. She thought that it made sense to lodge a claim now. I really did not want to know about making a claim. I think that, in my head, I was trying to put what had happened to me in a minor category. Putting in a claim would change that. Rosemary reassured me that I was entitled to make a claim. She pointed out that I was entitled to a lump-sum compensation and to ongoing financial assistance to help pay for the costs incurred by counselling.

I wanted to scream that the system should have protected me rather than compensate me after the fact.

I think that Rosemary hoped that a claim would help me to see the significance of what had happened to me. I never verbalised the horrendous feeling I had. Mr Black's abuse made me feel like a child prostitute who was now being paid for services rendered.

After completing and submitting the forms, I put the matter out of my mind completely. I knew that my revelations would be devastating to my family. I had been so brainwashed and programmed by Mr Black that I was convinced I was at fault for what he had done to me. Therefore, I was now determined to bury everything back down.

Besides, there was so much going on in the rest of my life that I was able to absorb myself in other matters. With my State Final Examinations rapidly approaching, I had a lot of studying to do on top of my ongoing shift work and assessments. I was terrified of failing State Finals, so I pushed myself to the extreme with my study. I was working long hours. Unfortunately, one of the side effects of long hours (and of my exhaustion) was the exacerbation of my nightmares. During the day, I busied myself by trying to remember large amounts of data for finals in order to stop my mind from remembering the past. At night, my sleep was disturbed and punctuated by the recurring nightmare.

I was eating poorly. Fortunately, my weight loss slowed. This was because my opportunity to exercise was significantly reduced.

One day, a lady at church pulled me aside to ask me what was going on. I told her little, saying only that I was stressed and working hard. We chatted about things. She was kind and caring. I mentioned that a couple of my friends were concerned about me. Also, I hinted that there was something else going on. She told me firmly that Christians do not have problems because we just give them all to Jesus.

For me as a Christian, the pangs of guilt, shame, and failure I felt after she said this were overwhelming. It was like physical pain. I remember smiling sweetly at the woman and saying that I guessed she was right.

But then I also knew that I couldn't confide in her anymore. There would be no more support from this quarter. Even worse than that, I now had an immense sense of failure in my faith as well. I really felt that I should have a better grasp on things.

While all of this was going on, I and my classmates were busy applying for graduate jobs ahead of receiving our exam results. I applied for dozens of jobs. This is not an easy task in the best of times. Now it was exceedingly difficult, given the state that I was in, how low my self-confidence was, and how very sure I had become that I would fail State Finals! Jobs for nurses were scarce at this point, particularly for new Graduate Nurses. That was another thing to worry about. By now, however, I was past worry and was simply petrified.

All the while, I was working hard to appear normal and to act like nothing was going on, juggling an ever increasing number of balls while trying to appear cool, calm, and collected. I was terrified that I was going to lose it at any moment.

State Finals were made up of two exam papers. Students sat for the exams on two consecutive mornings. The first part was a three-hour multiple-choice paper. The second was a three-hour-long answer paper. We all arrived at Canterbury University, a neutral environment, to sit the papers. Everyone was nervous and pretending that they weren't. We had been warned that neither paper was easy. We were told that we must take great care to read the questions thoroughly. We were advised to take great care in providing our answers.

After the first paper, some students were keen to compare their answers. I knew that this was unwise. I thought it was much better just to leave that paper alone and head away to relax as much as possible before starting the next paper. When I finished the second paper, I felt an immense sense of relief that it was finished and that there would be no more study – unless I had failed and had to resit the papers in six months' time. There would be a five- to six-week wait for results.

After all the work and study of the last three years, suddenly I had nothing to do. Everything came to a dramatic halt. After months of juggling balls, I was exhausted and scared. I really had no idea what was next – either what I wanted to do or what I would have to do.

Rosemary pushed me to take this time to work on myself, to reveal what had happened, and to rework my thinking on what had happened.

Very quickly, my life spun out of control. I was anxious, tired, afraid, and completely overwhelmed. I did not want to be told what I would have to do, and I did not want to do the work I was being told to do.

Christmas came and went. In the second week of January, my exam results arrived. I had passed. I was stunned. By now, I was so numb about life that I barely knew how to react. My family and friends were thrilled. On the outside I smiled, but it was all so superficial.

The arrival of my results meant that I had another round of letters to send out to the places to which I had sent job applications so as to inform them of my positive results. In the weeks following, I received letters of rejection and letters informing me that I was on a waiting list. This was not at all promising. I was, however, strangely numb about the job situation.

Rosemary had arranged to see me one last time at the end of January. Once Polytechnic started for the year in the following February, I would no longer be eligible to see her at the Polytechnic Health Centre. She was open about that and indicated that we would talk about my options when the time came.

On a Knife's Edge

I was drowning and I had reached the point where the thought of living and having to make decisions was completely overwhelming. I wanted out. I wanted the world to stop. I began to contemplate suicide. Even more surprising was that this thought didn't shock me at all.

A new Graduate Nurse I might have been, but I knew enough to know at least a little about what method of suicide was likely to succeed. I began to plan. At first, I made a "just in case" plan – just in case things started to unravel. Later, I moved into a different mind-set. I knew that I was going to go through with my plan.

I had been asked to house-sit for someone. I knew that this would give me the opportunity to disappear – to carry out my plan and not be found too quickly. It was completely sorted in my mind. My plan was detailed. I knew when, where, and how I would kill myself. I knew there was a very high probability that I would succeed. What a relief that was. It was sorted. No more worry and no more fear. All that was left to do was to count down the days.

Did I think of my family and friends? Yes. I was completely convinced that they would be better off without me and much better off not knowing the sordid details of my life. I was absolutely convinced that Mr Black's abusing me was all my fault. This meant that I was absolutely evil. If I killed myself, then I would be doing everyone a favour.

I had decided that I would take an overdose on a Tuesday morning in an isolated spot. I was to see Rosemary on the following Wednesday, but I would not be turning up.

Romy decided at the last minute that she would come and house-sit with me. This was a dramatic change. It threw me a curveball. I panicked. I wanted to follow through with my plan, but I knew that I couldn't do so with Romy there with me. And then what about Rosemary? I really didn't want to see her again.

My anxiety levels rocketed. I couldn't think of what to do. I decided that I couldn't follow through with my plan. I would ring and leave a message on the answering machine to let Rosemary know that I was unable to make the appointment, and then I would replan everything for a later date.

I rang the Polytechnic Health Centre very early in the morning, knowing that the machine would take the call. But when I rang, Rosemary answered the phone. I wanted to scream. I was so far beyond being able to be calm on the phone.

I stammered out that I wouldn't be able to make the appointment. Rosemary asked why. I couldn't lie to her, even at this point, so I simply said that I'd rather not say. The conversation was strained as she tried to work out what was going on and as I tried to give nothing away. She asked the question again and again. In the end, I asked her to stop.

"Suzanne, what is going on?"

"Nothing."

"Suzanne?"

"Nothing."

"Suzanne?"

"I just don't want to talk anymore. I have had enough."

"Suzanne, what do you mean by that?"

"I mean that I am tired and frustrated and I wish it was all over."

"Suzanne, what are you thinking?"

"Nothing."

"Suzanne?"

"I wish that it was finished, and I wish I was dead. I want to be dead."

"Suzanne, do you have a plan?"

"I have to go."

"Suzanne, I need to know."

"And I need to go!"

"Suzanne, you will answer me. Do you have a plan?"

"Yes."

"Oh no. Where are you?"

"It doesn't matter."

"Are you at home?"

"No."

"Where are you?"

"It doesn't matter!"

"Suzanne!"

"Don't worry. I can't do it. I had a plan and I was going to do it today, but my friend invited herself to stay with me, so I can't do it with her here."

"Suzanne, you need to come here now to see me."

"No!"

"Or will I come to you?"

"No! Don't worry. It will be fine."

"Suzanne, are you coming here, or do I come to you?"

"No."

"Suzanne, we need to talk. But if you won't, then I will need to let the police know that I am concerned for your safety."

"Oh."

The more she talked, the more anxious I became. Rosemary was certainly attuned to my anxiety now. It seemed that the more anxious I was, the firmer she became. I tried to persuade her that I would be fine, but it was like trying to negotiate with a brick wall! I knew she was not going to back down or be dismissed. O the frustration. I reached the conclusion that I was going to have to face her. I would have to talk to her. I agreed to meet.

Things moved very quickly now. Within an hour, I was in an office with a Psychiatrist who was the leader for the Psychiatric Emergency Services in Christchurch. He was kind, calm, and professional, but also caring. He had received a quick brief from Rosemary, enough to say to me that "Some horrible things happened some time ago, and now you are in a vulnerable position." Not interested in pursuing previous events, he cut to the chase very quickly and wanted to talk about how I was feeling now – and, of course, what I was thinking now.

Bear in mind that this was a man whom I had met during my training and whom I had seen at work in the clinical setting. I knew this man to be an excellent clinician and an astute Psychiatrist. I now found myself sitting in a sterile room with him, one-to-one.

I was defensive and was very unhappy about being in this position. In fact, I was angry, but I understood that it wouldn't be a good idea to show how angry I felt.

The psychiatrist asked me very direct questions in a firm and clear way. There was no avoidance and no distraction.

He asked what my plan was. I refused to tell him.

He asked if it was to be an overdose. I said yes.

He asked if I knew when. I said yes.

He asked if I knew where. I said yes.

He asked if I had the means to carry out my plan. I told him that if he was asking if I had the tablets that I planned to take, then the answer was yes.

He asked if I had the pills with me. I said no, mentioning that I was not quite that silly.

He asked if I would now reconsider my position. I said no.

He leant back in his seat and looked at me. Very quietly, he said that he would be back in a moment. He left the room. There was no time for me to think or leave, as he returned very quickly with Rosemary.

He explained to Rosemary that he had asked me a number of questions and that he appreciated my attempts to answer him honestly. Then he leant in towards me and spoke very quietly but firmly. He told me that he was very concerned for me and for my safety. He said that my reluctance to specify my plan to him left him in a position. He believed that if I was allowed to return home, then I would undertake to commit suicide. At this point, I looked him in the eye. I said nothing, but we both knew that he was right. He said that because I was a qualified Nurse, he thought that my chance of success in any suicide attempt would be very high. I looked at him again and raised my eyebrows.

He sighed and said that it was his professional opinion that it would be negligent and dangerous if he let me go home, even with good follow-up planned. He said, "We need to admit you in order to keep you safe. I need to ask you if you agree to that."

I was very angry and distressed at the thought. I said that I would prefer to go home now, please.

He smiled very kindly and told me that I couldn't go home. If I would not agree to be admitted for safety and observation, he explained, then there were sufficient grounds to legally commit me for treatment.

Wow – I had not seen that coming! I said, "No way!"

Now I was angry and defensive and very anti. The change in my demeanour was well picked up by both the psychiatrist and Rosemary.

Rosemary quietly asked me to reconsider. I said nothing. Again, the psychiatrist asked if I would agree to be admitted. I said nothing. He looked me straight in the eye and said, "You are a very intelligent young lady. In spite of the past, you have a lot going for you. I need to ensure your safety while you are in this frame of mind. I will prepare the papers."

I sat very quietly. There was simply nothing at all to say. A few more questions were asked, but I declined to converse.

I remember being asked if I would behave in the car on the way to the Psychiatric Hospital or if I would need a police car to take me. I was surprised by the question. Suddenly, I felt deflated. I replied that the psychiatrist and Rosemary had made a decision I didn't agree with it, but I said that I would comply. The relief in the room was palpable.

That morning, I had awakened feeling anxious and sensing that my life was falling apart. As I sat in the car on the way to the Acute Psychiatric Ward, it occurred to me that life had just got a whole lot worse – worse than ever.

I was anxious about what was ahead. As a student, I had been in the Acute Ward during placements. I knew very well what those wards were like. I had no idea how the staff there were going to treat me. Now I was just wishing that I had kept my mouth shut.

I knew that things were about to get ten times worse. Somebody was going to have to tell my parents, and they were going to be devastated. I felt such a sense of guilt. I felt responsible for what had happened to me and for what my parents were about to feel. None of this was what they wanted for me. I went from the high state of passing the State Final Exam to the low state of being admitted to a Psychiatric Ward. Great work, Suzanne.

On top of that, I knew that I had put Romy in a terrible position. She was my friend and had been loyal and caring through some of my difficult times. I had been difficult. I feared that I had landed her in it today. She was unaware of all that I had been dealing with, and she did not know what I had been thinking or planning. I knew that she would struggle on many levels with what had played out today. She would feel bad that she had not realised where my mind was. As a nurse, she would feel some guilt for not having made me feel better. But right now, I knew she would be very angry with me and would, quite rightfully, feel betrayed.

My head was pounding. I felt sick. I felt embarrassed, but I was also angry. It seemed like the short car trip was taking forever. Initially, I sat quietly, but as the trip went on, I became agitated. I think the driver was concerned that I was going to jump out when the car stopped at the traffic lights. At one point, the nurse escort looked at me, smiled, and said, "It will be OK. You are going to be fine." She sounded very sure, but I was not convinced.

Acute Psychiatric Wards, including Fergusson Clinic 3 (FC3), where I was now headed, are dreadful places. All external doors and windows are locked, so staff members carry keys at all times. Internal doors are also locked. The atmosphere tends to be grey and tedious. The décor is plain and bland. When I was a student, one of my peers commented that it was such a dreadfully depressing place. She said that if you were not depressed when you arrived, then you would be depressed before long. She wasn't wrong.

Most of the staff wore mufti rather than uniform. The thought was that the mufti make the ward feel less like a hospital and less institutional. They don't really help, though.

On arrival, I was admitted to the acute wing of FC3. This meant that all of my belongings were taken, including my clothes. I was gifted with hospital pyjamas, a nightie. I was weighed (amongst mutterings and raised eyebrows from the nurse), and my blood pressure and temperature were checked. I was asked for a urine sample. My blood was taken for tests.

The staff were friendly enough and asked me various questions but I said nothing.

I was deemed to be a risk to myself, so I was under close watch. This meant that I was confined to a small, bare bedroom. A member of staff was expected to sight me every ten minutes. I was to stay in my room, with the exception of visits to the toilet, which was less than ten metres away.

The bedroom I was in was a secure room with an external window that could not be opened. The door had a handle and a lock on the outside of the room only. There was a small window into the corridor so that staff could look in for their checks. There was a mattress on the floor on one side of the room, plus a blanket and a pillow. There was nothing else.

I felt humiliated and incredibly vulnerable. Again, I wished that I had just kept my mouth shut. I asked myself for the hundredth time, "Why did I ring Rosemary?"

After an hour or so, I was asked to go with a nurse to an interview room. I remember thinking, "Here we go." I was shown into a room with no windows. Along one wall was a large mirror. I knew, from my psychiatric placements, that this was a window to another room, from which more members of the team could observe.

This was to be a preliminary discussion. It was rather brief. To be honest, there was not much chat, as I was not ready to talk. I was anti. There was talk about my legal status in the hospital. I was a committed patient, which meant that I was the responsibility of the hospital and was under their care. I could not leave without their permission. That would be my status for two weeks. After two weeks, my status would be reviewed by a judge. He or she could then formalise my status (which would mean a stay of two years) or let it lapse (in which case, all my rights would be returned to me).

Other than that, there was little said during the interview. I was returned to my room for the night. I was brought a meal, but I ate nothing. I was not hungry and, in fact, still felt ill. The nurses in the acute wing were very unimpressed by my refusal to eat. They made something of a fuss. I was very unimpressed by the fuss. I just sat very quietly and said nothing.

It was an incredibly long night. I had very little sleep. The night was punctuated by the regular noise of doors being locked and unlocked. There were the sounds of conversations between staff, and somewhat unpleasant noises from some of the mentally unwell, throughout the night.

The Truth Must Be Revealed

Morning arrived with a change of nursing staff on duty. My breakfast arrived. Strange to say, the cold porridge and cold toast were not at all appetising!

At mid morning, I was invited back to the interview room. My heart was racing and I was very frightened. A sleepless night had not cured or lessened my anxiety.

In the room were already two gentlemen. In the most bizarre of situations, I was seated in a room with a male psychiatrist, a male psychologist, and a male nurse. I remember thinking, "Great." I wondered how I was supposed to feel at ease and talk to these men about anything. So I maintained my default position and sat quietly.

It was explained to me that new patients admitted to the ward were assigned to one of the team, i.e. Psychiatrist, Clinical Psychologist or Nurse, and that person would oversee my care. I had been admitted under the care of the Clinical Psychologist, a gentleman named Mohammad, who was the gentleman currently explaining the situation to me. As time went on, I would recognise that this was a divine appointment with God's fingerprints all over it.

Mohammad took the lead in the discussion. When he asked me questions ("How are you feeling?"; "Did you sleep?"; "Is there anything you want to tell me?"), I answered with a shrug of the shoulders or a nod or shake of the head. At one point, he smiled and commented that I did not say much.

Things changed all of a sudden when the nurse commented that my parents had been ringing and were keen to see me. My reaction was dramatic. I became agitated. Tears streamed down my face. I quickly said, "No!" The strength of my reaction was a surprise to everyone in the room.

Mohammad leant forward in his seat, looked me in the eye, and said, "Suzanne, now you tell me what you are thinking."

I looked at him for a moment. With a very shaky voice, I said, "I can't see them. I just can't do that."

"Ah, that is too difficult yet?"

"Yes."

"Then we will leave that till later. When you are ready, we will do that together." He looked at the nurse and said, "I will ring her parents."

O the guilt about how I was treating those who loved me. But I could not face them yet ...

The three men in the room exchanged looks. It was clear that they were considering what to do next. Mohammad tapped his fingers on the chair and said, "I think that is enough for now, but I think, Suzanne, that you and I will talk again soon. Is there anything you need?"

"I am really cold."

"We will see that you get a cardigan or sweatshirt."

I was returned to my room by another nurse. She took one look at me and asked, "That was rough?" I nodded and was happy to retreat to my hideous room.

Lunch came and went away. The nurse came and sat with me. "You haven't eaten anything since you arrived. I understand that you probably have lost your appetite. Is there anything at all that you could face?"

"No."

"Nothing at all?"

"No."

"Then could you drink more in the meantime? Suzanne, if you become dehydrated, we will have to move you to Christchurch Hospital for intravenous fluids."

I looked at her and nodded.

"Good girl!"

I felt very alone. I could not face my family or friends, even though I felt isolated. I wanted to think, but I was so tired and frightened that even thinking was hard work. I felt no hope at all. Part of me wanted to scream and tell everyone to go away and leave me alone. I wanted to tell them to shut up and let me think. But while sitting in that room during that lunchtime, I realised that the very best idea was just to be quiet. I was committed and there was no way out of the situation. I would be quiet and would just get through the two weeks.

In the middle of the afternoon, Mohammad came to see me in my room. "Hi, Suzanne. Come with me for a chat. Let's have a change of scene. We'll go to my office."

A change of scene appealed to me. Mohammad unlocked the door to his office and stood back to let me go in. I was struck by the contrast in his room. It was cluttered and there was so much colour! There were shelves full of books. Half of me wanted to peruse the titles. He indicated a chair, and I took a seat. Inwardly, I braced myself for what was to come next.

He asked if there was anything I would like to talk about. I shook my head emphatically. "Anything you need?" I raised my eyebrows and shook my head. "You really don't say much, do you, Suzanne?"

"No," I answered. He laughed.

It was quiet for a moment or two before Mohammad leant forward to say, "I think that you have a lot to say and a lot you need to say. I know some things, Suzanne, but I would like to hear you tell me your story." After a few more moments of quiet, he asked, "Shall I tell you what I know, Suzanne?"

I sat quietly, frightened to say anything in case I started and never stopped. I was afraid that instead of talking, I would scream. I was frightened of what he might say and of how it would all sound in someone else's words.

This time, Mohammad didn't wait for a reply. "I know quite a lot. I know that lately you have been talking with Rosemary about some horrendous things that an evil man did to you while you were a child in his care. I know that it has not been easy to talk about those things. I know that you have been sleeping badly and have been plagued by nightmares. I know that you have also had some significant stress in your life while you have been completing your training and sitting your exams. Congratulations on completing and passing!" I nodded my head.

"I know that things have become more difficult in recent days and that you put together a plan which would lead to your death. I know that your plan was foiled – thank God – and that you now find yourself somewhere you don't want to be. Against your will, you are stuck here, stuck in a room with a man whom you don't know and who is asking you to talk.

"I know some other things that you need to hear and I need to say. I know that you are an exceptionally bright young lady. You must be. To train as a nurse is tough, but with all of this other stuff going on, it is even tougher. Then to blitz your coursework with all of this – that takes brilliance. I know that you are a much loved daughter, as your parents have phoned a number of times already. I know that you are a nice person. The loyalty and care you receive from your family, from Rosemary, and from your friends indicates that you are special. I know that you possess an enviable level of self-discipline and determination.

"I know that things feel dark, overwhelming, and hopeless where you are right now, but I know that things will improve. Now it is your turn to talk."

"It seems that you know everything."

"No. I know a little. Tell me what you think and feel."

"Why? I have talked and talked. I know that it does not help."

"Ah, but you have not talked to me. I know that talking to me would help. I am good!"

I smiled and shook my head. He laughed. "Suzanne, we are going to do well. We will be friends facing the monsters together. Now talk to me, my friend."

"No."

"Ah, you will."

There was something about Mohammad that made me feel safe. His tone with me was far from patronising. He had given me much to think about, much to contemplate. I knew that I hadn't talked but I had let my guard down somewhat and I suspected that he knew that as well.

The following morning, one of the nurses in the acute wing was asked to take me to Mohammad's office. I assumed it was to talk, so I immediately tensed. However on my arrival there the Nurse stayed and Mohammad smiled and said "Relax. I will do the talking."

It turned out that there had been a team meeting that morning and I had been discussed at some length (there's a lovely thought!). Mohammad said that consensus had been reached: a diagnosis of post-traumatic stress disorder was right for me. It was linked to the childhood abuse that I experienced. He explained that there was some disagreement about the most appropriate treatment course for me.

The medical and nursing staff were of the opinion that I was also exhibiting signs of depression (low mood, loss of appetite, disturbed sleep, and moments of agitation). They determined that a course of antidepressants was in order.

Mohammad believed that psychotherapy alone would provide the best results for me. He said that the rest of the team were adamant that I should start taking antidepressants.

I held my breath. I understood the debate, and I understood the polarisation of opinion. I also understood the unspoken – that

Mohammad would have been put under some considerable pressure to agree and to start the treatment.

"I would like you to consider appeasing my colleagues by agreeing to a trial of antidepressants."

"I am a committed patient, so I am supposed to do as I am told."

"You are an intelligent, trained professional. I think you should be party to this decision."

I remember leaning back in my seat and wanting to laugh. This was just so very bizarre. The body language of the nurse screamed that she thought this scene was ridiculous and I suspect that she thought I would refuse the medication and then be made to take it. I also noted that Mohammad's demeanour was different today. I realised that this was no game to him. He wanted me to partake in making the decision.

"I am not depressed."

"No, I don't believe you are. Traumatised, exhausted, and haunted, but not depressed."

"I am opposed to taking medications unnecessarily."

"Yes, me too."

"Okay, I will trial them – maybe instead of talking!"

Shock registered on Mohammad's face and on the nurse's face.

"Of course, having said that, we have just negated any placebo effect!" He laughed and thanked me as I moved to leave the room.

As I got to the door, I turned, smiled, and said, "Instead of talking, Mohammad." He smiled and shook his head.

I wasn't happy about starting medication, but in my mind I had two weeks to show that I would be compliant and cooperative. Besides, taking the meds was more palatable than baring my soul through talking.

I took the first dose that night. Unfortunately, the meds do present side effects. I already knew that and could easily have recited the list of side effects, but there had been no discussion about them. Mostly, the side effects were a nuisance – dry mouth and so on. A couple of nights later, I got up to go to the toilet and fainted on the cold tiled floor. I came to, very cold and disorientated. The episode was unobserved. I assumed that the meds had induced a postural drop in my blood pressure, meaning that if I stood up quickly, my blood pressure would drop and lead to a faint. This was confirmed later when I mentioned the incident to Mohammad, who sent me for another medical check-up.

The same day that I agreed to the medication, I was called for a chat with Mohammad in the afternoon. I think he was optimistic that my cooperation with the medication situation would translate into a greater level of cooperation and openness to talking about things.

In my mind the two things were separate and I was not at all interested in talking.

Mohammad tried to open up a conversation, but I was resistive. All of a sudden, he changed tack.

"I need to talk to you about your parents. Suzanne, they are worried sick. They care about you. I think that you should see them."

"Oh?"

"Suzanne? So you will see them?"

"Yes, but let us be very clear: I am not telling them anything."

"Pardon?"

"I will see them, but I am not telling them what happened to me."

"Suzanne, seeing them is a great start, but they will need to be told."

"No!"

"Suzanne."

"I said no!"

"I think that we should talk about this."

"No. I think that I will go now, please."

"OK, Suzanne. OK."

A meeting with my parents was quickly organised. I was terrified. Just prior to my meeting with them, Mohammad came to see me. He knew I was scared and that I was dreading this. He tried to convince me again that I should tell my parents what was behind all of this. I was still adamant that I would not tell them. For the first time, Mohammad looked very frustrated.

Meeting my parents was awkward and uncomfortable – for all of us. So much had happened in the last few days for each of us. Mohammad took the lead in the conversation and talked my parents through my legal status. He told them what was happening in terms of my management and treatment.

There was awkwardness in the room. It was like there was a large elephant in the room that we all knew was there, but that no one was acknowledging. Everyone was trying to step around it. It was obvious to me that my parents wanted and needed to know more, but the professionals in the room were bound by my wishes to not say anything.

Up until this point, I had said very little. I had kept my head down in an attempt to be invisible. Now I looked around the room, listening to all that was being said. A break in the conversation didn't take long to materialise, as Mohammad was running out of things to say. He looked at me and raised his eyebrows.

I took a deep breath and said to my parents, "I think that we should just cut to the chase. This might all make more sense if I tell you that when I was at Primary School, I was sexually abused by a teacher and I have been unsuccessfully trying to work through it all."

There was a momentary pause in the room. I wanted permission to leave, but I wasn't cheeky enough to ask for it. I looked Mohammad in the eye. He nodded to me. He was clearly stunned, but he also looked relieved. I was surprised to see that my parents looked relieved as well.

My mother broke the silence and asked, "It was Mr Black, wasn't it?"

"Yes."

Mohammad looked surprised and asked my mother how she had guessed that. She confirmed that there had been reports of Mr Black's misdemeanours after he had taught me. She had simply put two and two together.

Unbeknown to me, my mother had talked to one of her long-time friends (a social worker by trade) after my admission to the psychiatric ward. This family friend had alerted my mum to the possibility that a history of sexual abuse could be behind what was happening to me now. My parents had prayed for a revelation of the truth at this meeting. Against my plans, that prayer was answered.

The rest of the meeting was less scary. Mohammad explained to my parents that he believed that I had post-traumatic stress disorder. He said that he was optimistic that I would do well. He tempered this statement with the warning that it would be hard work and that the process would not be short.

As the meeting finished, my parents asked if they could visit me more. Mohammad looked me in the eye and raised his eyebrows. I nodded. He said that he thought that was a good idea, that visiting would be helpful.

I was just very relieved that my parents wanted to return!

I was returned to my room, where I sat on the bed and sobbed. The nurse came in and tried to engage me in conversation, but I turned my back to her and cried.

That evening, another nurse came in to check on me and to talk to me. I found these conversations to be difficult even in the best of times. This day had been long and trying. The nurse really could not grasp that I did not want to talk. I didn't want to have a deep and meaningful chat.

She pushed ahead. She wanted to talk about my history, but I didn't. All of a sudden, she looked at me and asked, "How come you didn't tell anyone or report it? If you had reported it, then it would have been OK for the other little girl. I don't know how you can you live with that."

I felt like I had been slapped across the face. I was stunned. Nothing was said for a moment.

Then I looked the nurse straight in the eye and said as coldly as I could, "Well, I guess that you don't understand any of this, except maybe you understand how a paedophile thinks. He blamed me for all of it too, so I guess you would be on the same page as him. Have you forgotten already that I don't want to live? I think you should leave now."

She left. I wanted to cry, but I was weary from crying. I crawled into bed and pulled the blanket over my head and wished the world would go away.

The following morning, I asked to see Mohammad. As I was walked into his office, he smiled, said "Good morning," and asked me how I was.

I answered, "Fine."

He put his papers down and looked at me. "Well, Suzanne, do I sense some anger this morning?"

"Yes! I think with the utmost of respect that you should ask the nursing staff to leave any talking or psychotherapy to you and that I would appreciate it if they would leave me alone."

"Wow. What happened?"

I reported the conversation of the previous evening. Mohammad's face darkened. I looked him in the eye. "I am responsible for what happened to that other little girl; however, right now I have enough guilt to keep me occupied for some time. That nurse needs to back off. And, by the way, you should know that I am feeling increasingly uncomfortable here. One of the male patients is following me all the time. If I change rooms, he follows me. He has started making inappropriate comments. To be blunt, he is making my skin crawl.

I know he is ill, but I am feeling stalked. Even other patients are calling him my stalker."

"Suzanne ..."

"I'm not finished. While we are having this conversation, could you please tell the nursing staff to stop hassling me about food and eating? It is rather ridiculous for them to be trying to get me to eat more and lecturing me on nutrition when, quite frankly, I want to be dead."

He took a seat and then indicated another for me.

"Oh, really?" I said.

"Suzanne, I will follow up with the nurses on the points that you have raised. Believe me, I will be talking to them. I am very concerned about all of those things. I know that they are worried about your eating, because it is mentioned to me at least twice every day. I will tell you what I have told them: your eating, or lack of it, is a symptom of the underlying stress. It is not a problem in itself. I think if we work through some of the issues, then this will fix itself. The next thing, Suzanne, is this. Listen to me. The only person responsible for what that man did to you or to anyone else is him. End of discussion."

I looked at him. He looked at me and I started to leave.

"Do you want to respond to that, Suzanne?"

"No."

"No? Why not?" Frustration was etched across his face.

"There is no point. We have differing views on that. Given that we now know each other's opinion, there seems little point in talking about it more."

"Well, I have another question for you then. Where is your God in all of your thinking?"

"Pardon?"

"Oh, you heard me very well!"

It was a question that no one had asked me. No one had dared to go near the subject of my faith or lack of it. Yet, in the quiet of the night, it was something that plagued me. I had found myself unable to pray. Someone had given me a Bible, but I was unable to open it. And now this man had cut straight to the heart of the matter.

I looked at him and quietly replied, "I think that you, of all people, should not be asking me that question. Leave it alone."

He'd hit a nerve and he wasn't going to back away. "Where was God, Suzanne? Did he not care? Does he not care now? Was your God unable to help you then and now? What kind of God is this?"

He leant back in his seat and crossed his arms. There was something of a Mexican stand-off. The ball was in my court.

I looked him in the eye. "I don't know why God didn't stop it. I believe that he could have. I believe that he does care. This is not punishment. It is pain. No, he doesn't blame me or hold me responsible."

"Suzanne, if God does not blame you, then why do you allow that evil man to blame you? If God does not hold you responsible, then why do you hold yourself responsible?"

I stood and left the room without saying another word. I did, however, find that I could pray again after this conversation.

A short time later there were closed doors and some very intense conversations between Mohammad and other staff. From then on, the deep and meaningful conversations were left to Mohammad. My stalker was moved elsewhere.

From then on things changed somewhat. Mohammad introduced me to a young lady called Karelia who was nearing the end of her training as a Clinical Psychologist. He explained that I would be seeing her for most of my chats. This was a surprise and a significant change.

The Penny Drops Somewhat

For some days, I saw Karelia every morning for a chat. I think I should make it clear that although I refer to it as a chat, there was absolutely nothing relaxed and informal about it. It was hard work and intense.

I was keen to be allowed to go home. My Graduation ceremony was days away, and I was aware that nursing students were about to return to clinical placement – including the acute psychiatric ward that I was in. I believed that I was being compliant and cooperative. I also believed that I would be allowed to go to Graduation.

One morning when Karelia and I were chatting, she noted that I was a little distracted. She asked why. I explained that I was keen to go to my Graduation, but I was dismayed that no one was talking about it. She told me that the indication was that I would need to stay in the ward for another week or two. I was mortified. I asked if I would be allowed out for my Graduation. She said that she thought this was a reasonable request. She then said that she would ask about it.

Later in the day, Karelia and Mohammad came to find me. They explained that I was still considered to be high risk. There was concern that the Graduation ceremony would be too stressful for me. I would receive no day pass to attend my Graduation. I protested, saying that it wasn't fair and mentioning that I had done all that was asked of me and more.

Karelia and Mohammad were unmoved. I asked if I could go if I had an appropriate escort. They said no.

I left the room, slamming the door as I went. Once back in my room, I sat on my bed and cried. Karelia came to see me, but I refused to have a conversation.

Teatime came. I refused to eat. I would not speak or interact with anyone. I was very upset. Graduation had become a goal for me to look forward to, but now it was gone.

Medication time came. When I didn't present for my pill, a nurse came to find me. She cheerfully asked me to come with her. I did. She gave me the tablet to take. I held it in my hand and looked at it. I didn't want it. I didn't believe that it was what would help me. I had agreed to take the pills, believing that it was a sign of my cooperation. Suddenly, I didn't feel compliant anymore.

The nurse noticed that I hadn't taken the medication. "You have to take it, Suzanne. It is part of your treatment. You are committed. You must take it."

I looked at her, then at the pill, and then again at her. "I take them because I agreed to. Just maybe I am reconsidering my decision," I said. Concern flickered across her face.

I rolled the pill around in the palm of my hand. It was tiny. I knew that with one small swallow, it would be gone. But I was angry now.

"Suzanne, please take the pill."

I looked at the nurse again. Did I really want to make a battle out of this ridiculous little pill? She was already quietly summoning back up.

I opened my mouth and swallowed the pill.

"Have you taken it, Suzanne, or are you hiding it?" I opened my mouth and hands to reveal that the pill was gone. I turned quickly and quietly to leave the room.

I returned to my bed. A short time later, a junior doctor arrived to see me. "The nurses are concerned that you are more agitated tonight." I just looked at him. He offered me some anti-anxiety medication. I just shook my head. He left.

A few moments later, another nurse, Paul, came to see me. I knew him from my student days and actually had a lot of respect for him. He sat quietly beside me and asked, "Tough day?"

"Yep."

"Do you want to talk?"

"Nope!"

"You're a bit agitated."

"Yep."

"What are you thinking?"

"Don't ask."

"Why?"

"I can't lie to you."

"Good. What are you thinking?"

"OK – I wish I was dead. I want to be dead."

"Suzanne, you wanted to be dead, or you want to be dead now?"

"Yes and yes."

"Are you having thoughts of harming yourself now?"

"Yes."

"Oh, Suzanne. Do you have a plan?"

"Working on it."

"Come on – come with me."

"Where?"

"Just to the office."

Once we were in the office, phone calls were made. The decision was made that I should be returned to the acute wing for more close observation – "at least overnight."

Now I was really angry. I was asked to go to the acute wing, but I declined. I was assisted there by a couple of the male nurses. They held me firmly to the mattress while another nurse searched me.

At this point, things went from bad to worse. With a male nurse almost astride me, I had a massive flashback. Suddenly, I was ten years old and being held down by Mr Black. I tried to scream, but no noise came out. I tried to move, but I was firmly pinned down. Finally, I was able to say, "Please, no. Please, no."

Suddenly, Paul realised that there was more to my reaction and pulled the others away. He knelt beside me and said very quietly, "It is okay, Suzanne. It's okay. He isn't here, and you are okay." I sat, hugging my knees and sobbing.

It was a miserable, long night. I was angry with the world. I was even more angry with myself.

The next morning, I was quickly moved back to the ward and visited by Karelia, who invited me for a chat. I declined, as I was in no mood to talk. I added that the decision not to allow me to go to my Graduation was rubbish. She conceded that it was a harsh decision.

I had a quiet day, keeping to myself. I was very discouraged, as I really thought I had been starting to make progress. I felt that my efforts hadn't been acknowledged. Now I felt like I'd gone backwards.

Later that afternoon, I was visited by Mohammad, who sat quietly for a few minutes before saying, "You need to talk with Karelia, especially when things are harder."

"I don't want to talk about things."

"You need to talk about why you don't want to talk. You need to keep talking. The tougher things are, the more you need to talk."

"I am so tired and frustrated. I feel like I am talked to like I am a naughty child."

"I don't talk to you like that."

"No."

"Does Karelia?"

"No."

"And ..."

"I hate this place. I am tired of these walls and of being stuck in here. I am tired of aiming for something when I don't know what I am aiming for. No matter what I do, it is not enough."

"What do you want?"

"To go home."

"Not yet. What else?"

"To go to my Graduation."

"I can't change that decision. What else?"

"I want to get out."

"Fresh air?"

"It's a start!"

"Yes. I think that you should walk to Karelia's office for your chats from now on. You can go for walks or runs within the hospital grounds as much as you like, but you stay inside the grounds – yes?"

"Yes."

"I think we should organise some outings for you with your mum and dad. An hour or two at home. We'll work towards a weekend at home. Yes?"

"Are you serious?"

"Very. But you have to keep talking to us."

"Mohammad …"

"Yes?"

"I had a flashback last night."

"When they were holding you down?"

"Yes."

"Paul thought so and wrote about it in the notes. Does that happen much?"

"Yes … but never like that before."

"Are you worried about it? It is OK. Not pleasant for you, but it is just a sign that there are things at the surface now that need to be talked through."

Suddenly, the penny dropped. If I talked, then the staff could hear the alarm bells ringing for me – the ones that I had stopped listening to. It wasn't just about making me better; it was also about keeping me safe from myself in the meantime. I guessed they were waiting for my own alarm bells to reset. With that understanding came a glimmer of hope.

Just being in the ward had become very uncomfortable for me. I knew that there were team meetings wherein I was discussed. I also knew that there was chatter amongst the staff about me. I was different from the patients they usually saw. I think that, to some extent, there was some interest in what had led someone like me to this position. I also knew that Mohammad was advocating very strongly for me. I was so very grateful for that.

I loved going for walks. It was clear that the nursing staff were not convinced that it was a wise idea, but it was great for me to have just a little bit of freedom. Now I understood that talking about things didn't just mean talking about the sexual abuse over and over again. I found it easier to be more cooperative in this area too.

Gradually, I opened up more and more to Karelia. Some progress was made. When the judge visited, my legal status was changed. The reception order was allowed to lapse, and all my legal rights were returned to me. I could see progress, but I was frustrated by the slowness of it.

I had few visitors while I was an inpatient. My parents were concerned that when I was better, people's memory of my admission might become a stumbling block. At the time, I didn't really care about that, but I did worry that my parents were embarrassed by my appalling behaviour or by what had happened to me.

Mum and Dad visited regularly and were encouraging. Simon visited too, although he was clearly bothered by the setting. Still, it was great to see him. I remember one night when he arrived with a massive chocolate Humpty Dumpty for me. It was huge. For someone who hadn't eaten any chocolate for quite some time, I found it rather daunting. After Simon left, I laughed at the size of the chocolate. I took it to the lounge and shared it with the other patients. It was a wonderfully kind thought on Simon's part.

A school friend visited me. She was incredible. She didn't know why I was there and she talked to me like normal, about normal things. She completely ignored our setting until she was leaving when she quietly said, "It isn't much good in here, so get better really quickly!"

Romy was in and out. Things were strained between us at times. I am sure that I was immensely frustrating to her. She had been very frequent with her visits, but they suddenly slowed. I said nothing to her about it, as I felt I had no right at all to make demands on her or her time. One afternoon, she came in and suddenly said, "There is something I need to tell you. I know you are not going to like it." Always an introduction that would induce a "brace yourself" reaction.

She explained that she had met a chap through church and that they were dating. I was genuinely pleased for her and asked all the appropriate questions. I reassured her that I understood that she wanted to spend time with him.

I did understand. I was very pleased for her, but that night I prayed and cried. It seemed that my life was falling apart while Romy was falling in love. I had absolutely no interest in dating or falling in love, but the cruel irony hit hard: the hardest chapter of my life was happening during the happiest chapter of Romy's life.

I coped well with ever increasing amounts of leave. Just as Mohammad was talking about discharging me with outpatient follow-up, a letter arrived inviting me to a job interview for a staff nurse position. I was excited and terrified. I worried how I would present and if I could even do the job.

I talked to Karelia about it. We decided that the timing was excellent. When the time came round, I put on my best frock and headed to the interview.

Carving Out a Career

It turned out that I was the only person being interviewed for this job. It was less of an interview and more of a "when can you start" chat. Wow! This was what I had worked so hard for, and now it was happening. I was very scared.

I was discharged from hospital and sent home. My follow-up appointments with Karelia were to be weekly initially. Later, they would occur fortnightly. It was great to be home and to start work a week later. My being able to go and debrief with Karelia was an amazing safety net.

I did have to admit to Karelia that, on my arrival home, I found the pills that had been central to my suicide plan. I am sure that my parents had taken a look around for them, but they hadn't found them, as I had left the pills well tucked away. Poor Karelia was mortified. I laughed and said that it was OK, that I had gotten rid of them. Curiosity got the better of her, so she asked what they were. I smiled and said, "Just a deadly cocktail."

Everyone at home had to adjust to having me back. Those who knew where I'd been were watching me very closely. This was to be expected and was very understandable. After weeks of being closely observed, I was very keen to be allowed to just get on with things. I learnt at a later time that one of the nurses had told my parents that

I was likely to be in and out of hospital for the rest of my life. Given this information, my parent's caution was to be expected.

I was never really sure who knew where I had been and who didn't know. However, it became very easy for me to tell after a couple of moments with people who were uncomfortable around me and unsure of what to say.

On my discharge, there had been some discussion about what I should do if things started to feel like they were unravelling again. I was confident that I was never going to return to those dark days, but I took the staff's advice on board – complete with a checklist of things to look out for.

I blossomed in my job. My skills and confidence grew quickly – maybe too quickly!

At one appointment with Karelia, I took the bull by the horns and asked if I could stop taking the antidepressants. She was dubious, but I was insistent. After some negotiating with Mohammad and the psychiatrist via Karelia, I was granted permission to cease taking the medicine on the basis that I was doing well. Also, the medication had not done much for me.

I missed my regular chats with Karelia when they stopped. Still, I really was doing much better. During my final session with her, she asked me what had changed. I told her that one day I realised that I wasn't going to be allowed to commit suicide and that I was going to have to get on with living. I figured that if that was the case, then I should do a much better job of living. She smiled and said, "Those perfectionistic tendencies again!"

I experienced some interesting moments, such as the day when the psychiatrist from Psychiatric Emergency Services came to see a patient whom I was looking after. He talked briefly to me about the patient, read the notes, saw the patient, and offered his advice in the notes. I watched him work and decided that he had no recollection of me at all. This was not surprising, given the number of people he met during any given year. As he moved to leave the ward, he made eye contact with me, smiled, and said quietly, "It really is lovely to see you looking so well." Nice!

A short time after this, I was invited to the wedding of a couple of friends. All of my family were going. I was excited about the day. It was a lovely day and a very happy time for the young couple.

I still found it hard to be around so many people, though. As the evening grew later, I decided that I would head home. I had come under my own steam, so it would be easy to take myself home. I said my goodbyes and headed out the door. Dad and Simon offered to walk me out to the car, but I reassured them that I was fine on my own.

As I headed down the driveway, I was joined by Peter who just casually talked with me as we walked to our cars. Peter, at that stage, was working as a psychiatric registrar and yes, he knew about my admission to the psychiatric ward. He kindly offered his support and asked if there was anything I needed.

I remember him smiling and commenting that it might take family and friends some time to relax about having me at home – longer than for me. I smiled and said that I thought I had given them good cause to worry about me, so I wasn't about to complain about their concern.

We arrived at my car, which I unlocked. As I drove away, I saw Peter heading back into the wedding. I smiled when I realised that he had quietly escorted me to my car. I had just assumed that he was heading home too.

Work was going really well. It was a major adjustment and the pace of the work was fast in the busy medical ward, but I loved it and threw myself into things. I was always looking for opportunities to learn and to extend myself. In terms of church, I was unsettled for some time. I tried a few places for varying amounts of time, but I made no real connection anywhere.

Romy and Glenn announced their engagement, which came as no surprise to me. They added that they would be moving to Canada for a couple of years to enable Glenn to continue work on his PhD. There was a real sense that our lives were going in very different directions. I was asked to be a bridesmaid – actually I was told that I would be one. I was thrilled to do so. But I was not so thrilled about them moving so far away. I understood their decision, but I was sad about the prospect of my friend living so far away!

In my late teens, I had been diagnosed with asthma. It hadn't been a major problem previously. It flared up every now and again, but mostly it was well managed with low levels of treatment. However, this changed. Over the next year or two, my asthma became problematic and led to some admissions to hospital and increasing amounts of medications. My weight fluctuated with the corticosteroids that were now used to treat my asthma.

There was increasing frustration for both the Respiratory Physician and myself. I remember one outpatient appointment where we discussed what to try next. We decided that it was worth it for me to look at more allergy testing and I was subsequently referred to another doctor in the city. He was based in a General Practice, but he had a special interest in allergies and psychotherapy. I was warned that the initial appointment would be long and would involve a very detailed history.

I arrived eager for answers and suggestions. The doctor started with the obvious – looking at my asthma history and medications. Then we talked about the rest of my medical history.

There was a long list of "have you ever" questions and all the answers were no until he asked, "Have you ever been prescribed antidepressants?"

"Ah, yes," I replied.

I openly explained my use of an antidepressant. I also explained the debate regarding whether I had depression or post-traumatic stress disorder (PTSD). Of course, the doctor's next question was why the staff at the psychiatric ward had considered diagnosing me with PTSD.

My heart sank but again I answered honestly. The doctor asked how long I had undertaken counselling. He was unhappy with my answer: "Nowhere near long enough."

He immediately announced that the unexplained trigger wasn't an allergy. Instead, it was unresolved psychological issues. He said that I would need more counselling. He was a little derogatory about such an obvious link being missed. I sat a little stunned.

Then he announced that, given the fact that I was there, he might as well have a look at me. Once he lifted my top at the back to listen to my chest, he said with some surprise, "You have hives all over your back!"

"Yes."

"You didn't mention hives before!"

"You didn't ask about hives!"

At this point he conceded that there might be some allergy component and he put me on a bland diet. The plan was to gradually reintroduce foods to see if we could identify any problems with any particular foods. I was to return to see him in a few weeks.

On my return, I found that the doctor was even more adamant that my problem was psychological. He subsequently dismissed any other findings. He suggested that I make an appointment to see someone at the practice for counselling, naming someone whom he thought would be good.

I left the doctor's office with no intention of returning. I did, however, consider whether I needed more counselling. I was very sure that my asthma was not psychological nor that the triggers were psychological. I thought about the checklist that Mohammad and Karelia had given me. There were no ticks against their list.

A few weeks later, I had an appointment with my Respiratory Consultant. I had worked in clinical settings with him. Also, I had worked on community projects with him. He had looked after my asthma for a couple of years. I liked the man and respected him.

Initially, Chris and I talked about my asthma. Then he leant back in his seat and clicked his pen. This was usually a sign that he was considering something. Normally, he would suddenly announce what we should do next. This time was different, though. He kept looking up at me as if he wanted to say something but was unsure of what to say or how to say it. I smiled and asked, "Yes?"

He said, "I have received a letter and a phone call from our allergy friend."

"Right."

"Suzanne, why didn't you tell me everything?"

"Pardon?"

"He told me that you had an acute psychiatric admission because you were suicidal. He told me that you were the victim of significant sexual abuse as a child. Is that right?"

"Yes, that is right."

"Why didn't you tell me?"

"I didn't think that it was clinically relevant."

"Never mind clinical relevancy. I thought you trusted me as a friend."

"Chris, I am sorry. It wasn't a reflection on you. It is just something that I don't tell everyone. Not many people know, and fewer people understand or can cope with it."

"I understand that, but still ..."

"I am sorry."

"Still, it does leave us with a question that should now be addressed. Is this affecting your asthma?"

"No."

"Suzanne, if I am to be honest, I must say that I don't think it is either. But this is not my area of expertise. I think we should have a consultation with someone who is more likely to know."

"OK."

"Really – you are OK with this?"

"Yes. Let's look at it and take advice. Can I just ask that we are careful? I work in the system. The last thing I want is to be the centre of gossip and rumour."

"Indeed. So we have options …"

We brainstormed and came up with some options.

1. A referral to Psychiatric Services – I was concerned, however, that this was too close to home for me. I was working with these people. Chris agreed.
2. I could see one of the psychiatrists who had a private practice and who also did public work.
   Chris liked this idea less, as he was concerned about the cost for me.
3. We could seek out other, community-based options.

At this point, I had an idea, but it was a little out there. I offered a quick prayer before saying, "There is someone else, a doctor who is working in a GP practice in town who has an interest in psychiatry."

"His name?"

"Peter ____."

"Ah, yes, I know him. He is excellent, but would you feel comfortable with him? Silly question, Suzanne, but should we be looking for a woman?"

"It'll be fine. I know he would give an honest and frank opinion. But would his opinion help here?"

"Yes. Let's do this."

It was decided that I would make an appointment and then ask Peter to ring Chris to have a conversation about his findings. I was due to fly out to Canada for a holiday with Romy and Glenn in two weeks. Chris directed me to try to see Peter before I left.

As I prepared to leave the office, Chris looked at me. "Two things to mention. You understand that you have grounds for a complaint to the Medical Council. There was a significant breach of your privacy, and it should be reported. The information was yours to share and in the very least, he should have asked your permission to share it with me. The other thing is that I am glad I know about your history with abuse. It doesn't diminish my opinion of you at all. Just so you know."

I returned home and tracked down the phone number for Peter. Avoiding any procrastination, I rang and left a message asking him to return my call. I left my name and number.

Peter rang that evening. I started the conversation with, "I don't know if you remember me, but you once offered your help if I needed it."

"I remember very well who you are, and I remember offering you my help. What can I do for you, Suzanne?"

I took a big breath and explained very briefly why I needed an opinion for Chris: so he could determine whether or not psychological triggers were to account for my unstable asthma. Peter asked if Chris knew that I would be asking for his opinion. I said yes.

"So it sounds like we need to meet for a chat. I'm sure that you are really looking forward to that!"

The next morning, I rang the health centre for an appointment time. A few days later, I arrived at the centre with a few moments to spare and discovered that Peter was running a few minutes late. "Always does," the receptionist informed me with a smile. I flicked my way through a magazine and realised that I was nervous.

Peter was very kind and somewhat cheeky but we were soon down to business. He asked what had led me to seek his opinion. I explained about the allergy assessment and said that Chris had been told more of my history, at which point Peter raised his eyebrows.

He asked why I had never told Chris myself. I explained that really I had just got on with my life and I viewed the sexual abuse as a past chapter. I said that it was not to be hidden, but it was not necessary for me to proclaim it from the rooftops. I said that I, now with the benefit of my hindsight, should have told Chris, but in all honesty it had just never come up.

Peter asked more questions about my work, my family, my stress, and my asthma. He asked questions about how I felt now about my admission to FC3. Somehow, we covered a lot of ground in a short time. I didn't lose the plot at all. I felt calm and largely unconcerned about Peter's questions. I didn't even mind talking.

"Right, I will ring Chris and let him know what I think. But you should know what I think. I am very sure that whatever is triggering your asthma is not psychological. I will tell him that. However, Suzanne, I do think that there would be a benefit to you if you had some further counselling."

"Oh?"

"You have done remarkably well, but I don't think that the work is finished."

"Well, that is great news."

"I thought that you would be appreciative!"

I explained that I was flying out of the country in a week's time. Peter informed me that this was fine, as he would still be there when I got back! Then, somewhat more seriously, he told me that he thought that there was work to do. He said that he was very happy to work through the process with me. Following this, he mentioned that he would understand if I preferred to see someone else. He could recommend others if I was interested.

Oh, man! I thought this was all done. I didn't really want to do all of this again. Yet I knew that I was stronger this time. I also knew that if I was really honest, then I would have to admit that some of the work I had done was very superficial. I was tempted to say that I thought we should leave well alone while things were good, but I knew that I didn't want to return to those dark days ever again.

Decision made: I would do anything to avoid letting things get bad.

Peter had sat quietly while I thought things through. Now I looked up and smiled. "OK, if it needs to be done, then I guess I'd better get on with it. I have to warn you that I can be rather difficult!"

"Yes, your reputation goes before you! Don't worry. I'm not frightened!"

At that moment, I knew two things. Firstly, my instincts had been right about there having been discussion about me back in FC3. And Peter had heard it. Secondly, this was going to be a very different working relationship.

"I'll see you when I get back then."

"Indeed. Have a great holiday. But, Suzanne, make an appointment now, on your way out. We wouldn't want you to forget, would we?"

I headed home knowing that I had work ahead of me and that it might not be easy. But first things first. I would have to talk to Mum and Dad about it. I would lay all cards on the table, out in the open.

My trip to Canada was well timed. The long-haul flight to Hawaii was a great opportunity for me to think things through. I reconsidered the events since my time in FC3. Mostly, things had gone very well. My career was going really well. I had friends, and I had taken up some neat hobbies. Things were okay.

I thought about what Peter had said about the work not being finished. I thought about counselling. Knowing from experience that I hated that process, I really didn't want to do it again.

I thought about the description of me – a victim of sexual abuse. What a title! I didn't like that title. I thought about another title that had been used in hospital – a survivor of sexual abuse. I didn't like that one either. So the question in this was what a better title was. I did not want to be a victim or a survivor. I wanted to be a winner in spite of having been sexually abused. I wanted to be living a full life, one fuller than the life I had been living. I wanted more.

Quietly, I prayed for wisdom, courage, and perseverance to do what I needed to do. I prayed that God would keep me safe on the road ahead.

I had a wonderful holiday in Canada. It was brilliant to catch up with Romy and Glenn. We had a great trip from Winnipeg through to the Canadian Rockies and back via the American side of the border. We laughed and talked and talked.

In the last days of my visit, Romy and I had the opportunity to have a rather deep conversation. She wanted to know how I really was and how life was going for me. I was honest, telling her the good and the most recent developments. She was positive and encouraging. She did press me to commit to doing all I needed to – and to do it well.

I left Romy and Glenn reluctantly. I cried during most of the flight from Winnipeg to Vancouver. I had missed them. However I was ready to return home and I was resolved to do everything I needed to do.

Rewiring Starts

Seeing Peter for counselling was a whole new story. I was stronger this time, which meant that he and I could really get stuck in.

His style was very different from what I had experienced before, and he certainly didn't let me get away with much. Plus, he wasn't afraid to use every tool in the box. He could be confrontational. He could be very funny. He teased me at times, but he was always kind. He was never afraid to ask the hard or awkward questions. If he did not like my answer, then he would say so: "That's rubbish and ridiculous. I think you could come up with a better answer than that!" He wasn't afraid of me, and I certainly wasn't frightened of him.

Initially, I was a little concerned about shocking him, but I soon learnt not to worry about that.

I think that I re-entered the world of counselling a little naively. I thought that it would take a few months and then it would all be sorted. I thought that I would talk about something and sort it, and then that part would be finished. But my experience was very different.

I remember getting very frustrated with something and saying, "We have been here before. We have talked about it, and here we go again. We are going round and round the same mountain."

"Yes, but with a different perspective this time."

"You think so?"

"I know so."

"It all looks and sounds the same to me."

"Trust me, you have made solid progress here. Now let's get on with it."

Fairly early on in the process, I had a session with Peter where I just couldn't put into words what I was thinking and feeling. My frustration levels were rising. Suddenly, he looked at me and said, "You know, sometimes the women who come to talk to me say they pretend that I am an honorary woman in order to make it easier for them to talk. Don't know if that helps."

I laughed. "I wasn't struggling to pick words because of your gender. But thanks anyway. I'll bear it in mind."

I was very motivated. At home, I wrote in my journal and made notes in sketchbooks, complete with diagrams and flow charts. They often led to discussion the next time I met with Peter.

Later, Peter would say that counselling me was the easiest counselling he'd ever experienced because I was motivated. He might say, "Let's think about this," and I would run with the idea (most of the time). I would do homework between our meetings. He might have thought it was easy, but it was hard work for me.

At times, I would back off from something hard, which would make him push all the harder.

On some issues, it was a battle of wills and he usually won. Behind his back, I called him names. In fact, I gave him a nickname that was a complete expression of my frustration. He knew that I called him names and that at times I was cross and frustrated with him. In some ways, it was easier to direct my frustration towards Peter rather than at my history or at the process. Peter expected a lot from me. He expected me to work hard and to complete things to a high standard. At times, I was tempted to take shortcuts or to accept a lower standard, but he was relentless in advising me not to do so. I am grateful for that now, but not so much at the time.

My family were aware that I was having counselling again. I think that they wondered why I couldn't just pull up my socks and get on with it. I've pondered about that quite a lot.

I was told by a couple of professionals that when there is a gap between the event and the reporting of that event (and the counselling), the person requires a longer counselling period. It was indicated to me that because there was a significant gap (eleven years) for me between being abused and revealing it to Rosemary, it would be a long road for me when dealing with it.

One of the things at which Mr Black was good, was grooming and brainwashing me very effectively. It was like having the wiring in my brain rewired into a faulty pattern. He set a wrong pattern of thinking in my head, particularly with regard to my thinking about myself.

So that was me at ten years of age. My problem was compounded by the years where I kept it all a secret. That meant that the faulty pattern was solidified in place and that the other work of my adolescent and teenage years had been left undone or was built into the faulty pattern. So here, in my early twenties, I had plenty of repair work to do.

It is a bit like building a tower with Jenga blocks. At first glance, the tower looks okay, but, on closer examination, you realise that some of the blocks are not right. They are a counterfeit that looks like a Jenga block but that doesn't quite fit the same. Eventually it leaves everything else weakened. So one by one you change the blocks for the real thing, but it is slow work because each block must be checked: "Is this real or wrong?" When you make a change, you must take care to ensure that the change is right. You cannot remove too many blocks at once or else the whole tower will topple.

Each foundational truth I held about myself and or about life had to be examined, thought about, and discussed. There had to be a careful thought about the replacement truth: Is it true? How do I know it is true? Can I measure it in some way? Also, what are the implications of changing that truth? Often, a simple change of perspective on one thing would have repercussions in so many other places.

Another thing to remember is that while undergoing counselling, ordinary life is carrying on with all of the bumps and stresses that are a part of day-to-day life. This meant that my stresses at work or in relationships were amplifying what was happening in therapy and vice versa. There were times when I wanted to stop what was happening in life while I dealt with historical stuff, or vice versa.

For me, it became very apparent that I had lived life in a narrow emotional band. One effect of suppressing the massive pain and injury that I incurred from the abuse was my suppression of any extremes of emotion. I was never very happy, never very sad, never very angry, and so on. I numbed myself if I moved outside of the narrow band. I cannot criticise what I did to survive because, indeed, it was about survival.

I can say that starting to re-feel my emotions was like being on a rather large roller-coaster ride. There were times when I wished I could numb things again. But, then again, having lived all that time from age ten years onwards never feeling really happy or experiencing any real joy, I realised what a dry existence that was.

And so to work …

The Abuse

Obviously, this was the topic that had to take centre stage initially during my counselling sessions. Even when I was seeing Peter, it was very difficult for me even to start talking about the abuse I experienced. In many ways, it was easier to talk about it in generalities and avoid any specifics of what had happened.

I started to build a picture (bit by bit) for Peter of what Mr Black was like and the types of things he said or did to me. I will admit that I edited out the worst bits for some time.

Unwittingly, though, I gave Peter an accurate picture of a man who had deliberately and skilfully manipulated me. Mr Black had very successfully groomed me to a point where he could do what he wanted to do to me, with minimal risk that I would report it. It was not obvious to me at that point that this background behaviour in fact elevated the seriousness of his acts of sexual abuse.

I had to do all of this work step by step. There was no going from 0 mph to 60 mph in 10 seconds!

Peter was consistently sensitive in this area, but he was also consistently tough. My mind had ingrained conclusions or reactions to events. He challenged those.

If I would keep insisting on the ingrained conclusion, then Peter would gently chuckle and raise his eyebrows. This was very infuriating, but very effective!

Over time, Peter suggested a few very helpful things, which I tried.

The first thing was that he asked me to think about how I would react if I were in that position now – that is, if I were being treated that way now as an adult. I was able to consider what I might think or feel, but I must admit that I still didn't emotionally connect with my history.

I drew a chart to show my thinking.

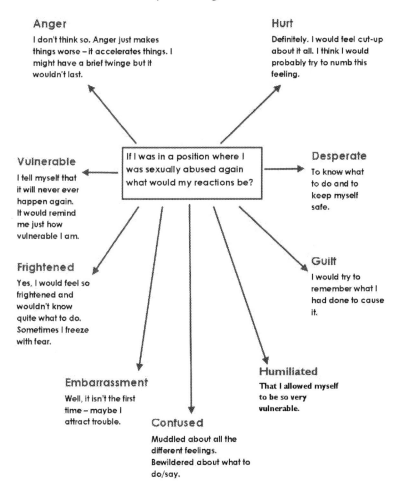

Anger
I don't think so. Anger just makes things worse – it accelerates things. I might have a brief twinge but it wouldn't last.

Hurt
Definitely. I would feel cut-up about it all. I think I would probably try to numb this feeling.

Vulnerable
I tell myself that it will never ever happen again. It would remind me just how vulnerable I am.

If I was in a position where I was sexually abused again what would my reactions be?

Desperate
To know what to do and to keep myself safe.

Frightened
Yes, I would feel so frightened and wouldn't know quite what to do. Sometimes I freeze with fear.

Guilt
I would try to remember what I had done to cause it.

Embarrassment
Well, it isn't the first time – maybe I attract trouble.

Confused
Muddled about all the different feelings. Bewildered about what to do/say.

Humiliated
That I allowed myself to be so very vulnerable.

The second thing that I tried with Peter's prompting was picturing that what had happened to me was happening to another child. This proved to be exceedingly powerful and emotionally wrenching. I could immediately see the horror of the abuse that I had suffered. I could understand how another child would feel. On an emotional level, I connected with what had happened to me more directly and more intensely than at any previous time.

The third thing that I tried was to research child sexual abuse. Even at this stage of counselling, I remained very dismissive of what had happened to me in terms of its seriousness. I was increasingly concerned that I and others in my life were overreacting to it. In fact, my dismissiveness became more intense after I had emotionally reconnected to my history.

In my head, I thought that because I had talked in generalities, Peter didn't really know what had happened. I remember saying to him, "It wasn't so bad. I'm just making a mountain out of a molehill."

"Would you like to hear my assessment?" he asked.

"No!"

"Thought so! I'll tell you anyway."

He went on to say that at the time, it was one of the worst cases of abuse that he had heard of. He said that Mr Black's skill in manipulating me, and how he had treated me, was incredibly severe and serious.

Peter's comments that day left me inwardly stunned. I felt extremely sick, and I cried all the way home.

What Peter had said was confronting, yet I knew I couldn't argue with his interpretation. He had most of the facts, and the facts that he didn't have would have only darkened the picture further.

I resolved to do some research into child sexual abuse. I needed to see for myself how it fell into the scheme of things. I found it to be harrowing work and rather distressing. Even more distressing was coming face-to-face with the reality of what had happened to me and what Mr Black would have been charged with, had I reported him.

Finally, I was able to gain some ground in this area. One day, I made a resolution with three decisions:

1. I am not responsible for what Mr Black did to me.
2. What he did to me was significant. I will not minimise it.
3. It does not matter how important or unimportant I think or feel I am. The fact remains that what Mr Black did was awful.

Of course, this led to implications elsewhere. I knew that I would have to adjust my view of myself.

There were other implications regarding my relationships with other people. So far, I had told few people of my history and those people whom I had told, had been told very little. Was that a right choice? Should they know more?

I knew by now that secrecy only helps the abuser and further disempowers the victim, and yet I knew that I was struggling to deal with telling anybody else. So subsequently I made a case-by-case decision about who to tell, when to tell them, and how much to tell them. Mostly, I haven't told people. When I have, I've mentioned only a very little.

Peter asked me to consider formally reporting what had happened. In fact, he offered to accompany me to the police station! I think this was an additional attempt of his to drive home the seriousness of the situation. I declined his kind offer. It did, however, make me think. I was very sure that the police wouldn't take me seriously, whereas Peter was very sure that they would.

I had nursed alongside a young woman who had made a career change to join the New Zealand Police. I arranged to catch up with her over coffee.

We chatted about things in general before and then I asked her to give me an opinion. Sharing my history with her, I explained that I had been undergoing counselling. Then I asked her about historical reporting of childhood sexual abuse.

She had listened to me somewhat stunned, but now it was her turn to speak. She said that my report would be taken very seriously indeed – and with the utmost sensitivity. What's more, she encouraged me to make the report and also offered to be there with me!

In all honesty, I gave considerable thought about whether or not to report Mr Black. I ultimately decided not to. The ramifications of being sexually abused had taken me to the brink of suicide once. On a number of occasions since, I struggled under the weight of it. I doubted that I had the resources to cope with a trial. Also, I did not want to put my family through that process.

I also wondered how it would be seeing Mr Black again and how I would react. I wondered further what that would be like in a courtroom setting. That was a frightening thought. I resolved not to report the incident.

There have been times when my decision not to share my story has left me feeling incredibly dishonest. At times, people have made assumptions about me and my life that have left me scratching my head.

I remember trying to support a friend through a tough time. One day, she looked at me and said, "What would you know? You with your goody-good life and your perfect family. What would you know about life's pain?" Ah …

There have been times when I have been left wondering if those I have told understand the gravity of my history. I remember spending a day with a friend. We were chatting as she was flicking through a newspaper. In the paper was a report of a sexual assault on a young woman. My friend exclaimed how terrible that was. I concurred. She went on to say that if she were sexually assaulted or raped, then she would have to kill herself. I sat very quietly, waiting for the penny to drop. It didn't. In the end, I muttered something about there being a way through sexual assault. Afterwards, I wondered whether my friend had forgotten my history or whether I hadn't spelt it out clearly enough for her.

Loss

Re-examining the events of my childhood led me to feel a tremendous sense of loss. In my mind, I felt that Mr Black had won. I wrote about it: "No matter what happens now or in the future, he will in some ways always have won."

> He took from me some things I could never get back. I lost some things I can never replace. Therefore, to some extent, Mr Black has won.

> He took my childhood and drove me into an adult world that I knew nothing about.

He took my innocence.

He took my trust in people.

He took my simplistic view of the world.

He took my simplistic view of myself.

I lost a year of my childhood.

I lost a chance to grow into adulthood at my pace.

It doesn't seem possible for me to change the balance of things. It doesn't seem important, either. So, if Mr Black wins, who cares?

I think there was incredible sense of loss, as I said before. I also grieved about how things might have been had I not been abused. The loss had to be worked through and acknowledged. This was the start of that process.

Did Mr Black win? No! I'm not sure that he really got away with it, either.

I have also come to realise that there were (and still are) plenty of people who cared about me.

Constant Reminders

Have you ever noticed that something strange happens when you buy a car (or shoes or a handbag)? You might have noticed that make and model of car on the road before, but when you buy one, you become aware of how many there are. Everywhere you go, everywhere you park, you see cars like yours.

This was a little like what happened for me. It seemed that whenever I opened the paper, I read about sexual violence; whenever I watched TV, I saw something about sexual assault; whenever I picked up a book, I read about sexual assault; and so on. All of these things served as a trigger to remind me.

There was another, more personal reminder for me. Mr Black had often talked to my class about his friend. They had met at university as students and were great friends. He told us stories about their adventures together at university. His friend had, and in fact still has, a high profile in Christchurch. Every time I saw Mr Black's friend in the news or around the city, a wave of fear and childhood memories flooded back to me.

These types of reminders, such as news reports of sexual assault, can still take my breath away today, but now I remember to pray for the injured party. I also offer God my heartfelt thanks for the progress I've made in my life.

The Pain of Those Memories

Feelings

As I said earlier, when I first started talking with Peter, my own feelings were rather blunted. It was an artificial way for me to be going through life. I needed to feel more emotions and learn how to deal with them. Some feelings returned more easily than others. Some were certainly more pleasant than others. Some were linked to the process rather than to the historical events. Still, bit by bit, these feelings needed to be welcomed and worked through.

Isolation

I had known isolation previously, the feeling that you are all alone and that no one else really understands you.

To some extent, that was true for me. However, I had to really rein in this thought. When I followed this emotion, it led me to increasingly isolate myself, which, in turn, compounded the feeling. Feeling isolated keeps you separated from others and keeps you quiet – really, there is no one to talk to.

It must also be acknowledged that the grooming that the teacher had put me through had really promoted the idea that no one would understand me, that everyone would blame me, and that no one would even believe me. An isolated victim is insurance for the abuser. My sense of isolation had only increased over time.

In the end, I had to challenge my feelings of isolation by reminding myself of the people around me who understood at least some of what I was feeling and who cared enough to stick close to me.

It took great courage and determination to push myself to build close relationships with others.

Fragile

Sometimes I just felt fragile. It would seem like the world was closing in and I was falling apart.

I learnt to recognise that feeling fragile meant that I should be kind to myself, but I also learnt that I sometimes used my feeling of fragility as an excuse to avoid working on something that I did not want to confront or deal with. Over time, I discovered that I was, in fact, much tougher than I thought I was.

There were times when my feeling fragile came with the fear that I was unravelling and headed back to FC3. Peter was always reassuring that I was doing well, that I was strong, and that things were different now.

Feeling fragile was also a helpful feeling. It felt like there were alarm bells going off in my head, which meant that I was well on the way to resetting those alarm bells and their trigger points.

Being Stuck and Experiencing Frustration

Sometimes I just simply felt stuck, like I was working so hard and getting nowhere. I wanted change in my life so much. I wanted things to be better, but I felt stuck in a place where I didn't want to be. I was searching and working to be somewhere better, but I felt stuck!

This was an ongoing problem, one that was really only helped by learning to trust Pete more – to know that he would push me when I needed it. Still, sometimes I just needed to consolidate the progress I had made. It was vital for a long time to trust Peter's perspective and his honesty about the progress I was making.

Anger

By this point there had been some anger, but this was, by and large, linked to the process and to the individuals who were helping me with the process. Not to the original abuse.

When I had been seeing Peter for just a little while and was starting to see the seriousness of what had happened to me, I became aware that he was pushing me and seemed to be trying to provoke me. One day, I said to him, "I think you are trying to make me angry."

"Yes."

"Why?"

"You're not angry about all of this? About what he did to you?"

"No."

"No? Then, yes, I would like to see you get angry about this."

So here I was. I had been living in an emotionally blunted state. I did not like or enjoy feeling many of the emotions, but it was anger that I most wanted to avoid.

I remember sitting and thinking about anger and my reactions to it. What did anger mean to me? I wrote a chart about my reactions to anger. Then I sat and stared at the chart. I was stunned as I looked at it. I understood now why I was avoiding anger.

I knew there was a link. On the day of the very worst abuse, I had become angry with Mr Black and was momentarily defiant. He then sought to teach me a lesson. My anger had led to a significant deterioration in the situation.

I was resistive to Peter's attempts to provoke me to feel angry. I did manage to keep the lid on my emotions for some time. I really didn't want to get angry. In my mind, it was overwhelming. and I thought that it would only make things worse.

However, I could leave the lid on my anger for only so long. As I examined what had happened to me and the seriousness of it, the pressure under the lid grew. That was very scary. I remember Peter pointing out that the lid was going to come off and that maybe it was possible for me to gently release the lid rather than wait for it to explode. He was right. Exhibiting a great deal of trust, I allowed him to help me lift the lid. Wow!

There was such emotion and such feeling. I was angry with the man, about what he did to me, about what he did to my childhood, about where his abuse took me, about how he messed with my mind, and about the fact that the abuse had been undetected. I was also very angry with myself.

The initial wave of anger was totally shocking, as I had known it would be. For me there were waves of anger for some time. There was another development that was equally as uncomfortable: other things in life would trigger an angry response. I found myself overreacting to situations.

I was a grown woman who was now learning how to feel angry and how to react in an appropriate way. I freely confess that I frequently failed in the latter. As the years have gone by, this has continued to be an area of challenge for me. I have required the great patience of others, and I have learnt to be very quick to apologise. I have gained some great skills, but, alas, I remain a work in progress.

My view of anger now? When I look at what I wrote about anger, I still understand it completely. Outbursts of anger can be like that. Unbridled anger can be a very dangerous thing.

I do, however, now understand that it is possible – in fact, essential – to develop tools and strategies for coping with anger and using it appropriately. At times, anger is a very appropriate and reasonable reaction to a person or a situation. It is, however, a feeling. As such, we can control anger rather than having it control us.

I have learnt that anger can be a very empowering and motivating emotion. Directed in a healthy way, it can lead to huge, positive changes in areas of social justice. Directed in an unhealthy way, it can lead to the mistreatment of others or even of ourselves.

Guilt

There was also the feeling of guilt. As time went on, I felt tremendous guilt: guilt about not reporting the abuse earlier and guilt about being suicidal and being prepared to take my own life.

In time, guilt led me to prayer. I repented and told God that I knew that what I had contemplated was wrong. I knew that I was forgiven by God, but it took me time to realise that I must also forgive myself.

Nightmares

For me nightmares became a signpost of how things were going for me. They were certainly a key trigger that led me to a point of revealing what had happened to me and to seek help.

As time went on, I became aware that the nightmares would return when I was particularly stressed, having to deal with something particularly intense or when I was just plain overtired. They also recurred when there were news reports of the abuse of other children.

Although I use the word *nightmares,* I experienced, in fact, only one nightmare, which was the replay of a scene from my childhood. It was like watching the same scene over and over again. I would awake in something of a frenzy with my heart racing, completely disorientated.

There were nights and weeks without a nightmare but at its worst I could have the same nightmare a number of times in one night. It would always take some time for me to resettle and to be able to sleep. Some days, I performed on very little sleep. At times, I absolutely dreaded going to sleep, which is never a good start to a night's sleep.

A couple of people had suggested that I could manipulate the dream in order to change what was happening. For instance, if you are being chased by a scary monster in a dream, then you can change the dream so that the monster is in fact Elmo wanting a hug. Or you might find a door to go through that the monster can't fit through. I did try this technique, but with no success. I have always wondered if I failed in my attempt because my nightmare was a flashback to a real event rather than something fictional in my head.

Peter suggested that I keep an object or two beside my bed that could help me to re-orientate myself after a nightmare. I tried this with some success by keeping my nursing medal beside my bed, which may seem rather strange. The medal was something linked only to my adulthood, and it certainly helped to calm me more quickly. Nevertheless, my nightmares remained an ongoing battleground.

During those years, I had returned to the New Life Centre and had joined a home group. My nearest group was led by Don and Ruth Ferguson, who were on the pastoral staff at the New Life Centre. I built up something of a rapport with them, particularly with Ruth. I was even brave enough to share some of my story with her. She was incredibly kind with her support. At one point, I shared with her my battle with nightmares.

She listened. After a few moments, she said, "I think we should pray about this." And so she very quietly prayed – no fireworks, nothing dramatic. Really, I thought no more of it.

A couple of nights later, I awoke during a nightmare. I remember feeling very frustrated. I sat up in bed and put the light on. "Okay, Lord. We have prayed about this. I need your help with these nightmares. Lord, I need to sleep. I believe that you give rest to the righteous. I believe that I am righteous through what Jesus did for me on the cross. Please, Lord, intervene with these nightmares. Amen."

I turned off the light and settled back into bed. Some time later, I fell asleep. Then the nightmare started again (groan!). This time, as the scene played out, it changed. In my nightmare, as Mr Black held me down, I turned my head to the side. There in the corner of the room was Jesus standing. He was crying. He was there, sharing my pain and my tears. I awoke, but without anxiety or disorientation.

A few days later, I shared the experience with Ruth. We sat in her lounge with tears rolling down our faces. It seemed to me an amazing answer to our prayer, but it also told me much more: Jesus knew, and he cared.

I would like to say that was the end of my nightmares. While it was a turning point, it was not the end. I had fewer nightmares and certainly not the clusters that I had had previously.

The nightmares were (and are) often a clue that something was (or is) up. I learnt to give some thought to what was behind my terrible recurring dream.

Me

It is fairly obvious that at some point I would have to take a look at myself and examine my own self-assessment.

Mr Black had been brutal in his psychological abuse of me. The names that he called me illustrated his brutality. He was a clever man who demolished me brick by brick until I believed that I was everything he told me I was. I took all of his words and his assessments, and integrated them into my thinking.

Another lesson that I had effectively learnt during the year that I spent in Mr Black's classroom was that life was much better for me if I went under the radar. If I behaved perfectly, then I would not draw attention to myself – and Mr Black might not even notice me. Maybe I would have always had perfectionistic tendencies, but that year certainly confirmed that I did.

Fairly early on when I was seeing Pete, I wrote down a list of how I saw myself.

- I am naughty and disobedient.
- I am responsible for awful things.
- I am stupid/slow.
- I am lazy.
- I am mean and selfish.
- I am disorganised and always in a shambles.
- I am forgetful.
- I am scruffy and everything I do is a mess.
- I am a liar and not to be trusted.
- I am unlovable.
- I am fat and very ugly.

There were a couple of other things that ought to have been on the list, but my courage failed me at that point, so I didn't include them.

I remember Peter's reaction once I read my list. First, he laughed and said, "You must be joking. If you were to write a list that is the antithesis of you, this would be it."

"Actually, I was serious!"

At this point, he became very serious and just kept saying, "This is so wrong."

Homework was set! I was to rewrite the list but in the opposite, and I was to justify the new position. "Give examples that show the opposite is true. If that is too hard to do, pretend you are writing down what I would say," Peter instructed me.

I returned for the following week's session having not completed the homework, which was unusual for me. I used my best distraction skills to direct the conversation elsewhere. Initially, I had some success. Halfway through the session, though, Peter asked to see my homework.

"What homework?"

"Good try, Suzanne! Where is it?"

I confessed that I had not done it, but I made no excuses. Peter smiled and picked up a pen. Quietly, he worked down the list, writing his perspective succinctly under each bullet point. Then he handed the book back to me. I read his points. Ouch. I wanted to argue the point or, rather, each point, but I decided it would be more prudent to bite my tongue and let the moment pass.

A few months later, Peter asked me to have another look at the list. I was to rewrite the list in a more positive manner, or at least write what I thought Peter would say or like to see. Ouch! It must be pointed out that Peter noted my discomfort and left me to enjoy the feeling.

I returned the following week with the homework – well, sort of. Peter was quick to note what I had left off the original list. He read what I had written and then said, "Much better!"

"Problem is, though, that it simply isn't true," I replied.

"Oh, Suzanne! It must be true if I would say it!"

"I don't believe what you made me write!"

"Ah, but you will."

The list was revisited over time and each time I would acknowledge where there were changes and admit that I had made progress. It has remained easy for me to have self-doubts, but even now I check myself on those thoughts. Sometimes I can hear Peter's voice echoing in my head: "You must be joking!"

At times, I have struggled with other people's expectations. It did seem that so very much was expected of me and, at times, demanded of me. I guess that my perfectionistic tendencies had led people to have high expectations of me in terms of work and life in general.

I often wondered what people would really think if they knew me better.

There were (and are) times when I was keen to be free and relaxed about things. I wanted to be having more fun.

As time goes on, I am realising that it is more important to be who I am. If I meet the expectations of others in the process, then that is all well and good. But if I don't, well, then maybe their expectations were unrealistic.

One of the truly wonderful things to come out of my healing process and particularly my time in FC3 was the realisation that I had to be authentic. I had no energy to be a different person in different settings or with different people. I just had to be me.

Men

I guess that it will come as no surprise to you to learn that I wasn't fussed on men! I remember Peter asking me about men one day. Very quickly, I retorted, "But, of course, all men are villains!"

"What?"

"You heard!"

"Ouch!"

"Nothing personal, of course."

"Well, thank you, but …"

So This was another area for me to investigate. Peter and I revisited my thoughts and feelings about men on a number of occasions. With time, I moved from disparaging "all men" to "all men except a few," eventually conceding that only some men are villains.

In all seriousness, though, I remained wary of men for some time. Sometimes I was right to be wary. I remember explaining to Peter a situation that had developed at work. In telling the tale, I stated that I didn't trust one of the men with whom I worked. I said that he made my skin crawl. I looked at Peter and said, "Sorry. There is just something about him." I remember that Peter smiled and told me that I must always trust my judgement and use my discernment. He pointed out that to dismiss one whole gender would be wrong, but he said that my antenna was accurate and that I must listen to it. Sometime later, there were revelations made at work about the man in question. Indeed, my antenna had been right on the mark.

I do trust my antenna. I must say that there have been times when I have erred on the side of caution, but I have never regretted it.

Many of my friends were dating and getting married during the years when I was in counselling. Initially, I was not even interested in dating. As I healed and as my attitude changed, I did begin to wonder if marriage would be part of my future. Marriage looked to me like such a minefield. I knew that I should wait until I was really ready before I even contemplated dating.

An Extraordinary God Is Revealed

God

I had become a Christian at a young age and although I didn't have a crisis of faith as such, there were a number of points that I had to work through in order to reconcile my faith with what had happened in my life.

There were things that I knew about God, but there were things that just didn't quite add up.

God protects his people and keeps them safe.

o   Why didn't he keep me safe? Where was his protection?

God loves me and cares about me.

o   Why didn't he halt what was happening when Mr Black abused me?
o   Does God love me less than he loves others?

God has a plan for my life, a plan to bless me.

o   Was the abuse part of God's plan? If not, then why did it happen?

God only allows us to face things that we can cope with.

- o   Yes, but what I have had to face has often felt like too much to me.

God can heal physical, emotional, and/or psychological pain.

- o   Why doesn't God take my pain away?

I had many questions. I will own that even acknowledging those questions was a hurdle for me. How can I question an all-powerful, all-knowing God? At a deep level, I felt angry with God. For some time, I felt abandoned by him.

Angry with God? Who could contemplate such a thing? One day, a family friend who was in ministry told me that God was big enough to cope with my being angry with him. This person encouraged me to tell God how I really felt, including my anger.

So I did as my friend suggested, all the while remembering to be respectful of the awesome God.

It is safe to say that I didn't like what had happened (or what was happening) to me and that I was feeling alone. To unload all my thoughts, feelings, and even doubts was such a relief. I didn't experience any bolts of lightning, however.

I know from reading Scripture that God takes the mistreatment of children very seriously. I know that he loves me very much, even when I don't feel it. I know he cares for and about me. I know that he does have a plan for me and that his plan for my life includes some amazingly good things coming out of the evil that I encountered. God didn't make the abuse happen. I cannot hold him responsible for it, just as he does not hold me responsible for it.

It seems that when I desire to be more than a victim or a survivor of abuse, I am in fact anticipating the healing hands of God as he carries out his work in my life. I have the reassurance that what he started in me, he will bring to completion. It is not my work or my striving that brings me to a point of healing. It is God's love freely poured into my life.

When I look back over my life, including the good and the bad bits, I can clearly see God's fingerprints all over it. The right people were around me at the right times. They whispered words of wisdom and encouragement to me at opportune moments.

Smudged fingerprints show when I have been resistant or have had tantrums, but fingerprints are there at all times. I still have questions and there are any number of things that I simply don't understand. Every now and then there are new insights and aha moments. I have learnt to trust God again and to trust his plan for me – and yes at times I do still protest about things.

Forgiveness

I must admit that mostly I didn't give much thought to forgiveness for a long time. Looking back I am not even sure why that was. It was pointed out to me by a number of people over time that things (feelings, thoughts or memories) come to the surface when they are ready to be dealt with, and in the best order for dealing with them. I did find that to be true. I also found that when things came to the surface, they could not be ignored.

I remember one Sunday morning when Don Ferguson preached about forgiveness. Obviously, this was not the first sermon I had heard on this topic, but that morning it was like Don had taken aim directly at me and then let loose. Of course he hadn't. In fact, at that point, he did not know my story. The text to which he was referring was the Lord's Prayer, especially "forgive us our sins as we forgive those who sin against us."

I had grown up in church circles. I knew the Lord's Prayer by memory by the time I was six years old. I had said this line time and time again but as Don expounded on those verses, I became increasingly uncomfortable in my seat and more than a little hot under the collar. How could God expect me to forgive Mr Black?!

On Tuesday of that week, I had already arranged to meet with Don's wife, Ruth, for coffee and a chat. Over coffee, I raised the subject of Don's sermon and mentioned how it had unsettled me. Ruth smiled ever so benignly and suggested that I chat with Don about it. At the time, I was not at all convinced that was a good idea. But on reflection, I decided that I would like to talk it through.

I met Don at his church office later in the week. I knew Don and Ruth well by now, so I wasn't nervous. I had assumed that Ruth would have shared with Don some of my story and my concerns about his sermon, but this was not the case. So I shared the rough outline of my history and my reaction to his sermon.

He told me that whenever he preaches on forgiveness, he is aware that for two or three people present, the subject will be particularly difficult. He told me that, bearing my history in mind, he found it very difficult to tell me that I must forgive Mr Black.

That made me feel a little better! However, he then said, "Let's talk about the theology of forgiveness." He asked me to explain to him what I knew of forgiveness.

I said that I believed that forgiveness was extended when repentance was present. So when someone is repentant or sorry and asks for forgiveness it is then extended or given to them.

At this point, Don told me that my theology was very faulty! He offered to walk me through it. Fundamentally, forgiveness is extended first and independent of any remorse or apology. When there is repentance the forgiveness is received but it had already been extended. When we look at the gospel, particularly at the crucifixion of Christ, we see that forgiveness was extended to all. Two thousand (or so) years after Christ was crucified, I repented and received forgiveness for my sins. God's forgiveness was there and was extended to me. It was already available to me when I became aware of my need for forgiveness.

The penny had dropped. I knew that I had no argument with what Don was saying. I looked him in the eye and said, "So I have to forgive Mr Black."

"I can't tell you that you have to, but …"

"But the Scripture tells me that I must?"

"Yes."

"Oh dear."

"Suzanne, it is a process. It is not about feelings. It is a decision to forgive in spite of the feelings."

I battled this issue for twenty-four hours before I made a very deliberate and considered decision that I would choose to forgive Mr Black. It seemed that now I knew that I was directed to do this by Scripture, it would be disobedient of me not to do so.

I prayed. I told God that I didn't feel like forgiving Mr Black. I said that I felt wronged. Nonetheless, I chose to forgive him. I saw no lightning bolts, no fireworks, but I knew that this was a massive step forward for me. I understood that forgiving Mr Black was not saying that what he did to me was alright. It was forgiving him and extending mercy. It was indeed a process. On a few occasions, I have restated my decision to forgive him.

Strangely, although I had extended forgiveness to a man, I felt that I had also released the burden of being abused to God. In a world that often seeks revenge for evil deeds, I had no need for revenge. The matter was (and is) all in God's hands now.

Relationships

During this whole process, some challenges arose in my relationships.

Obviously, my family and a few very close friends were aware of what had happened and knew that I was having counselling. Let me make it very clear that it is tough to see someone you care about go through all of this. I was blessed with people who cared about me and who did try to support me. Not at all easy when you are unsure of how best to support and when the person can be grumpy, withdrawn, or suddenly pleasant at any given moment – or all three in a short amount of time!

I felt a constant tension about what to say and how much to share. My need to talk about being abused was largely satisfied by having the opportunity to talk to Peter. I was determined that therapy, guidance, and any in-depth discussion about things that had happened to me should remain inside the counselling setting. I knew that it would be foolish to muddy the waters by receiving conflicting opinions and advice.

By and large, people were very respectful of that. What I did need was support during my healing process. Rewiring my thinking and confronting my emotions about my history (and the repair process) was emotionally and mentally exhausting work. I needed distraction and fun. I needed understanding. At times, I needed space. Trying to work out what I needed at any given time wasn't always straightforward for me, let alone for anyone else.

At times, I was incredibly self-focused and selfish. There were times when I had to remind myself that it wasn't all about me. It was easy to become egocentric in my thinking and behaviour – a trait that parents of teenagers will recognise. I would have to remind myself that I needed to be a good friend.

I did feel for my parents. They had always been of the mindset that a person should never mind counselling and just get on with things. Here I was now, requiring counselling – and intensive, prolonged counselling at that. To my parents' credit, they encouraged me to see it all through and were generous in their assessment when all was done.

I think for my parents, and also for Romy (especially), there were times when they were frustrated with the length of time that my process was taking. They all wanted Suzanne back. So did I!

I lived with a huge amount of guilt in regard to my parents and Romy. I felt guilty for putting them through the shock and concern that they were confronted with upon my admission to FC3. I felt guilty for having kept secrets for too long – not just about my history, but also about how bad things had become. I felt I had let my parents down by not coping better. I also felt that I had disappointed all of my family and friends by not living up to their expectations.

Bearing in mind that I had deferred most of the work that I should have done during my teen years, I was now also finding myself having to attempt to do some of that work. I needed to become more independent and more self-reliant. This can be a bumpy process for even the best of teenagers, and it was bumpy for me now. Added to that, I had given my parents real cause to be cautious and concerned.

So their concern for me was high as I was trying to grow into an independent young woman. Yes, that did create tensions.

In many ways Peter took the role of a coach both in my counselling and in other developmental changes. I healed from the damage caused by the abuse as I completed developmental work faced by teenagers. Personally, I can recommend a coach for teenagers. Peter would remind me to be kind. At other times, he would prompt me to be firm. More than anything, he encouraged me to maintain an active sense of humour!

Of course, as time went on, I was changing and growing as a person. Someone once described to me the after-effect of my process, saying that it was like having to meet and get to know a new Suzanne. At the time, I thought that was a little over the top, but there was also some truth in it. I became surer of my own opinions and reactions. Instead of keeping quiet, I was more likely to state my own opinion. I was more assertive. Some things that previously I would have just let slide, I now would put my foot firmly down about. It was hard for those closest to me as I changed. At some stage, they all had to let me move on from being an injured soldier to being a healed young woman.

At the same time, I was making new friendships. Some of those relationships were truly amazing. In some ways, they were easier friendships, as these people took me as I was at that point. Mostly, I did not even tell those friends about my complicated history. My experience was that sharing that information changed things dramatically. In some ways, my new friendships were refreshing and less complicated. Yet I always had a sense that I wasn't being quite honest or quite authentic.

Time and experience have taught me to be open and to share my history with friends, but to be particularly sensitive about the timing.

Always a Complication

As I progressed and put my life together, I noticed another change. I guess partly because of my age and because I was surrounded by friends who were getting married, my friends started to play matchmaker for me. Mostly, their efforts were light-hearted and not particularly serious. I would usually just laugh off their attempts to set me up with a man.

Part of me was becoming interested in dating and finding someone special, but mostly I was very content with my life. My career was taking off, and I was in a place where I was making peace with myself, my history, and the world.

On another day, I met Ruth for coffee. It was a lovely day. I remember sitting outside a busy café, enjoying great coffee and a lovely chat. Out of the blue, Ruth said, "I really do wish that you'd find a nice young man now. It would be lovely to see you settled with someone."

"Would it, now?"

"Yes, and I've been giving this some thought. I think that you and Pete would work well together."

At this point, I was at serious risk of choking on my coffee! "Ruth, put that thought right out of your mind. That is not going to happen."

"It could, with a little encouragement."

"Ruth, no! I have a professional relationship with him and it has to be left there. Full stop!"

"But maybe later?"

"No, Ruth. It can't happen. Besides, he would drive me nuts. And I would most certainly drive him nuts too!"

I swiftly changed the subject; but I was however left with a dilemma and a number of questions.

1. Do I seem desperate to have someone in my life?
2. How far had Ruth meddled? Does Peter know about this?
3. Was I giving off the wrong signals about my relationship with Peter?
4. Did I tell him about the conversation with Ruth?
5. What will happen if I don't tell Peter and Ruth meddles further?

When I next saw Peter, I was still in conflict about how to handle this situation. Reluctantly, I decided that it was wisest to tell him about my conversation with Ruth. I mean, I had already told him so much about myself. This was just another thing to mention …

"That would never happen, Suzanne," Peter said once I finished speaking.

"I know, Pete, and I made that very clear to Ruth."

There were a few awkward moments after this conversation, but not as many as I had feared.

Not long after this, Peter challenged me, saying that I was holding back on something. He wasn't wrong. There was a subject that I wanted to talk about and, in fact, needed to talk about, but I just couldn't quite do so. He suggested that maybe an appointment or two with a woman might help. I knew I wasn't going to ever approach the subject with him, so I agreed to see the lady whom he suggested.

It was awkward launching into something very personal with someone whom I hadn't met before. Five minutes into the chat with the female counsellor, I knew I wasn't going to go there with her either.

The woman and I talked for some time about my counselling with Peter, about the progress that I had made, and how I now found myself unable to open up about something.

"Suzanne, you have quite an unusual relationship with Peter."

"I guess."

"Suzanne, I must ask, are you having feelings about him?"

"Pardon?"

"It does happen when you are seeing someone regularly and sharing such personal information with them."

"Oh, for goodness' sake!"

"Would you like to explain your frustration with that question?"

"No!"

"Oh!"

"I guess that I do have an unusual relationship with him. Maybe it isn't a typical doctor–patient or counsellor–counselee relationship. I think that if it had been, then I would have made less progress. How do I see him? As a trained professional who is a friend. I guess I talk to him like he is an older brother. There is nothing else going on, and I have no desire or interest in there being anything else. If there had been any other feelings, I would have stopped going to see him. I respect him as a person and as a professional. That is all.

I understand that there are limits to a professional relationship. I would not ever contemplate crossing those lines."

"OK."

"Besides, on a very human level, he can drive me nuts."

I remember finishing the session and thinking, "Oh my goodness! What signals am I sending?"

The next time I saw Peter, he was interested to know how things had gone when I met with the other counsellor. I remember blushing and giggling, which didn't let me off the hook at all! So I told him about my appointment with her, albeit an edited version. Peter asked if I had discussed the issue that I had been avoiding.

"No!"

"Suzanne!"

"I couldn't."

"Suzanne! Are you going again?"

"Never!"

"What happened?"

"Did she ring you?"

"No. Suzanne?"

"I didn't want to talk to her about it. I can tell you what I am avoiding talking about, but with the understanding that *I don't want to talk about it!* Deal?"

"What did she talk with you about, then?"

"You and how we have an unusual relationship. She asked if I was having feelings for you!"

"Oh dear."

"'Oh dear' is right! For the record, no, I don't have feelings for you. I tried to explain that I see you more like a brother than as a potential date, but I don't know if she believed me. And, actually, I don't care if she did or not!"

"Right."

"After having had that conversation, there was absolutely no way that I could talk to her about what I had been avoiding!"

"Which is?"

"Stuff!"

"Suzanne!"

"Oh, for goodness' sake. I have been avoiding talking about dating and how to cope with flashbacks."

"Oh."

"Well, I couldn't talk to her about dating, feelings, personal space, and the potential for flashbacks when someone is in my personal space. I really couldn't talk about intimacy and stuff. She talked about our relationship. What was I supposed to say then, that I'd like to talk about sex?"

"I see. We could talk about it."

"Oh, don't even go there!"

As I was leaving that day, Peter very quietly said, "I think that when you are ready to consider someone, those things won't be an issue. Trust yourself."

For the record, Peter would have driven me nuts in any other capacity than as my counsellor. He was an amazingly kind and supportive professional. He was very skilled and yet so very real. But, shh … don't tell him!

Life Still Went On

In the background, my life was chugging along, with a thread of counselling weaving through my life's events. There were some challenges, but some amazing things were happening as well.

In terms of my career, initially I worked on an adult medical ward. As a new graduate, I found it to be an interesting ward to work on. It was a very busy acute ward which, in many ways, was under-resourced. There was also a lack of good nursing leadership. Having said that, I will now say that there was great camaraderie amongst the team. I was very much thrown into the deep end, and expected to swim. I did swim, but there were some rather scary moments. The job stretched me. I developed some solid skills – nursing skills and life skills. I was very fortunate when one of the senior staff nurses took me under her wing.

After seventeen months of my employment there, the ward was affected by restructuring. I moved to a second adult medical ward. It was a massive contrast. The work was similar, although the ward specialties were different and very interesting. The charge nurse was a great leader. She had built a great team on the ward. She was very empowering. Very quickly, I was presented with opportunities to learn specialist skills and leadership skills and to represent the ward on hospital committees. I thrived. I loved it. To cap it off, I made some great friends.

My next move a few years later was one I made somewhat reluctantly. I knew that I needed to stretch my clinical skills again and that I wanted a new challenge, so I moved to the Neonatal Intensive Care Unit (NICU). In some ways it was like being a new graduate all over again. I started just as the unit became incredibly busy, so once again I found myself being thrown in the deep end. I loved the work and I thrived on having a new specialty to learn. Before long, I was being given opportunities to be involved with more specialist skills. It was an area of incredible highs and incredible lows for me. The NICU was a place of great victories, but also of some tragic losses.

Unfortunately, the NICU had a reputation as being a home to bullies – and it was a reputation well deserved, unfortunately. I think that because I was a quick study, conscientious, and fairly quiet, I was able to avoid the attention of the worst bullies. I think that it also helped that my mother was working elsewhere in the Women's hospital and was well respected. Nonetheless, I saw the effects of bullying. On a few occasions, I witnessed bullying. I am pleased to say that I stepped in to stop the behaviour.

Amongst the team were some amazing people. I considered myself fortunate to work with them and to count them as my friends.

My self-confidence grew. My achievements in clinical settings translated to other areas of my life. I enjoyed meeting a cross section of people. It felt very good to know that I was making a difference in the lives of others. I was, however, still a work in progress. On some days, I would cringe during moments where I just knew that I could have handled things better.

By my mid twenties, I had reached a point where I wanted a little more independence. I considered going flatting, but at the back of my mind I preferred the idea of buying my own place. I had money saved and decided that this was the option that I would pursue.

I set to looking around at houses for sale. As usually happens, there was much more available just out of the price range that I had set. I found a few possibilities. Eventually, I found a small bungalow set back from the road down a long driveway. It was about ten years old. While the house itself was small, it was set on a large garden, which was well laid out. Once up the driveway, I really did feel that I could be anywhere. I confidently announced to my parents that the house didn't need anything done to it. The only problem was that it was about $15,000 out of my target range. I knew that the bank would almost certainly lend me the extra. After a lot of thought, I decided to walk away from the house and keep looking at what else was on the market. A week later, when I received a phone call from the estate agent, I learnt that the family who owned the bungalow were relocating. Their need to move had become more urgent. The man's employer had offered to pay half of the difference between the asking price and what the buyer paid. The estate agent asked me if I was still interested. Yes, I was! I arranged to view the house again. This time, I took my parents, my brother, and his girlfriend.

A second viewing confirmed that I really was interested. I made an offer, conditional on being able to put the finances together and a few other necessary details. The sellers made me a counter-offer, and I accepted it. I felt that the agreement should be fair to both parties. Indeed, it was. Within two weeks, all was confirmed.

Although I had said that the bungalow didn't need anything done to it, I decided to redecorate most of the house. The day after I took possession found Dad and me stripping wallpaper and sanding like crazy people. It felt wonderful. It was great to let my creative side go wild!

Simon had been dating Debbie for a while. I asked her if she would like to come flatting with me. I had geared my finances so that I did not need flatmates, but this seemed like an arrangement that might suit us both.

A side effect of having my brother's girlfriend as a flatmate was that I saw an awful lot of him too! He ate with me and Debbie on a number of evenings each week. My mother joked that I should charge him rent as well! Instead, she started sending him round with groceries.

Over the next year, I had a couple of other flatmates – with varying success. It became obvious to me that although I might get on with my flatmates as individuals, it doesn't necessarily follow that they will get on with each other!

Life is not all plain sailing for any of us, really. At one point, my family were rocked by the news that the son of a couple who were family friends had committed suicide. It was a family whom we had gotten to know quite well through church. Earlier, we'd laughed and said that they were our doubles. They had a daughter close in age to me who was also a nurse. Their son, similar in age to Simon, was also in banking.

I arrived home from work late one afternoon to hear the news. The young man, Daniel, had committed suicide at his flat while his girlfriend was at work. My parents were now at the family's home, actively supporting the bereaved parents. The police were coming and going. At one point, the police indicated that they needed someone to formally identify his body. Daniel's parents were in no shape for the task, and his sister was out of town. My mum was needed to stay where she was, offering support and comfort. It was decided that my dad would go. My mum wanted someone to go with him, so I offered to accompany him.

I will be very honest: it was gruelling. Nursing had meant that I cared for people who were dying and that I supported their families, but this was different. This person was young and had been full of life, but now he was gone – and by his own hand.

The police took my dad and me into a small room to view Daniel's body. I knew that this had thrown my dad somewhat. Daniel looked very different. I quickly and quietly said, "Yes, that is Daniel."

The policeman looked at my dad. "Sir?"

"Yes, that is Daniel."

The following days were dark and agonising for all. Grief was overwhelming for Daniel's family and for their close friends.

My mother was horrified that I, having been suicidal myself, had helped to identify Daniel. For me, that wasn't the difficult part. The difficult part was that I was knocked about by the immensity of the grief around me. I had contemplated and planned suicide and, in doing so, had dismissed any thought of the grief that I might cause. I thought that no one would care, but now I knew differently. Now I knew that it would have been devastating had I killed myself. The grief around me was heavy, but the burden of guilt I felt was smothering.

Yet I also had the realisation that, for whatever reason, God had intervened for me in such a way that my outcome was very different from Daniel's. I didn't really understand why God had intervened for me. Why not Daniel as well? I recognised the frailty of life. I could see how very far I had come.

At Christmas, my brother proposed to Debbie. Life was about to change again. The wedding date was set for January of the next year – the height of the New Zealand summer. Dresses were made and details were coming together. The house was full of wedding plans. Simon was around even more of the time! Deb asked her two sisters and me to be bridesmaids. I must admit that I was ambivalent about playing the role.

This wedding hit a sensitive note for me. Simon was my younger brother by two years. His bride was younger still. I felt like I had endured years of pain and hard work while all was great for them. This was true, and it felt unfair to me. I felt rather sorry for myself, shedding many tears in the week prior to their wedding. I'm sure that they were oblivious to my struggle. I was very relieved one day when my mum said, "This must be tough for you." It wasn't as if I was desperate to be married. I just wanted some good stuff to happen in my life, or so I told myself.

Simon and Debbie's wedding day was lovely. All went very smoothly. Simon had become a great friend to me over the years. We often had long conversations with each other. I knew that things would change from this point, but I also knew that the newlyweds were very happy and in love.

A Divine Matchmaker

A short time after Simon and Deb's wedding, another friend of mine announced her engagement. My mum suggested that I catch up with her. She told me that Nicki had an interesting story that I should hear. I will admit I was a little intrigued, so I invited Nicki around for a meal. It was a very interesting evening as she talked about what had been happening for her. She had been interested in meeting a young man (someone special), so she had joined a group for Christian single people. It was a national group that provided a pen pal list for people to get in touch with each other, not just for dating but also for friendship. For those who were interested, there were also groups that met locally for social activities.

Nicki had ended up being in contact with a man who lived in Wellington. One thing had led to another, and now they were engaged to be married. "You should join" were her parting words to me. She gave me the information about joining, which I quickly shoved into a drawer, putting it out of the way. Out of sight, out of mind.

Except it didn't really go out of mind. I was in a peculiar position, as most of my friends were married or had partners. Increasingly, I was left with the choice of going to the movies by myself or not at all. I found that I was spending more and more time by myself. I was feeling lonely and somewhat isolated. I knew I had to do something to increase my circle of friends, especially Christian friends.

After a great deal of thought about Nicki's suggestion and with a decision that was swinging in the breeze, I decided that I had nothing to lose. I pulled the envelope out of the drawer and sent off a letter to join the group.

A few days later, a large envelope arrived. In the envelope was a letter of explanation and a long list of people's names. Each name was accompanied by a brief description of the person. It all felt very strange. It took me twenty-four hours to even muster the courage to look through the list. It felt very weird to be reading about other people. Initially, I decided that I would wait and see if anyone wrote to me. However, once I read the list, one entry stood out, so I decided I would write to the man. He was Paul, who lived in Wellington. I am not even sure why his entry stood out except that I thought he sounded interesting and had a variety of interests.

I wrote a letter to Paul. The club had a system for mail. Members could send letters to the club, and the staff would forward the letters on. This meant there was no need to give out my own address initially. With Mum's encouragement, I erred on the side of caution and sent my letter to Paul through the club.

Over the next few weeks, I received a number of letters and replied to them. I was curious to see whether Paul from Wellington would reply. He did. It was a great letter. I suddenly realised how much one can pick up from a letter.

Judging by his first letter, it was obvious to me that Paul was clever and that he had a great sense of humour. He gave me a hard time for not including my own address, so I replied with my address, offering the explanation that my mother was concerned that I might be writing to an axe murderer and had encouraged me to send my letters through the club.

Over the next few months, I went on dates with a couple of the chaps I met through the club. I must say that, by and large, my dates were terrible. It became obvious that I wouldn't keep writing to everyone on the list. It was soon clear whom I should write to: Paul.

Paul and I settled into a pattern of writing to each other regularly. His letters were typed (Paul is a computer scientist by trade), and mine were handwritten. I looked forward to his letters. We shared the events of our week, and we shared our thoughts about and reactions to a huge range of subjects. His letters always had a question or two (or more). Usually, I answered the questions in my next letter, but sometimes I would ignore a question that I found awkward to answer. The letters were friendly and fun. Bit by bit, Paul and I were getting to know each other.

Then one week a letter arrived with something of a surprise. Paul was soon to be taking a holiday. As part of his holiday, he would be passing through Christchurch. He wrote that he would like to meet up, asking me, "How about it?" Well, my heart certainly missed a beat. The letters were wonderful, and I was enjoying our growing friendship. But if we met up, then that meant a date. My dates had been far from successful. Yet, at the same time, I was a little intrigued to meet Paul and see what he was like face-to-face.

It turned out that he was biking from Wellington (well, Picton) to Invercargill and would be overnighting in Christchurch. I explained about my nursing shifts for that week and sent him my phone number so that he could ring me when he arrived.

Paul had worked out when he expected to arrive in Christchurch. Sure enough, that day I received a phone call. We arranged a time for me to meet him at the camping ground where he was staying. So it was all going to change, one way or another.

I felt physically sick when driving to collect Paul. I was very nervous. Halfway there, I realised that I had no idea what he looked like! I was going to the main entrance of a camping ground to collect a man whom I didn't know – and I didn't know how to identify which one was Paul. Great!

I pulled up, stopped, and looked around. To my horror, I saw quite a number of people around, mostly men. I got out of the car, muttering quiet prayers under my breath.

A slim, red-haired man made his way over. He smiled and said, "Hi, I'm Paul." Phew! I must say that the red hair was a surprise, as was the beard. At least he didn't look like an axe murderer.

I had decided that it would be great to head to an Italian restaurant in the centre of town. It was a twenty-minute drive that seemed to take forever. Paul was very quiet. I was paranoid about my driving, as I knew that Paul worked in road safety. I was to find that his actual job was working as a computer scientist for the Land Transport Safety Authority which meant using his skills in writing software with a particular view to statistical analysis. At this point I was just worried about my driving.

The restaurant was busy. Paul and I were seated at a table for two right in the middle of the room. We each studied the menu and made our selections.

It was now that I discovered just how quiet Paul was. He was very quietly spoken and was no great conversationalist. I felt like I was trying to make conversation. Although he responded, he, by and large, left me to drive the conversation along. I was nervous, and the slowness of conversation was only making my nerves worse. I giggled too much, and I knew it. Our meals arrived and were delicious. Their arrival made the gaps in the conversation easier to navigate.

The thought of sitting there and trying to make conversation throughout the evening and over dessert did not appeal to me, so I suggested to Paul that we take a walk through the inner city. It was a great idea, as the pressure to talk eased with our walking. After a while, we ended up elsewhere for an enjoyable dessert.

The drive back to the campground was just as quiet. I remember thinking, "Well, that was a disaster. I won't hear from him again."

When I next saw my parents, they asked me how things had gone. I told them it was terrible! Mum asked what Paul was like. I reported that he was very nice and very quiet, saying that I thought that he was not my type. When I went to bed that night, I reflected that I was going to miss his letters.

A week later, I arrived home from work to find a phone message from Paul on the answering machine. He was now on his return trip to Wellington and would be in Christchurch overnight. He wondered if we could catch up again. Now, I wasn't expecting that. I was very surprised. I had no idea what to think or how to respond. It seemed polite to return his call. Again, I was surprised that he was really keen to get together. This time, there were complications with my shift work.

In the end, Paul decided that he would meet up with me at my church on the Sunday morning before I went to work in the afternoon. I am embarrassed to admit that I was uneasy about this. My perspective was that our date had been a disaster. And now to have him meet me at church – oh dear. I knew there would be an interrogation to follow, courtesy of my church friends.

Things worsened from there. That day happened to be my birthday, and my family had arranged to take me out for breakfast before church. My mother was furious that I hadn't invited Paul to join us for breakfast. Oh, I couldn't think of anything more uncomfortable for either of us.

At this point, I was attending South City Christian Centre, but my family were attending church elsewhere. In the middle of breakfast, my mother let the cat out of the hat by announcing that Paul was going to be meeting me at church that morning. An interrogation followed. My family all announced that they would be coming to church with me this morning! Oh no!

Sure enough, they all headed to South City for church. Paul was waiting when I arrived. He presented me with a birthday card. I was impressed that he had remembered my birthday. I introduced him to my family. As we headed into church, my mum leant in and whispered, "Oh, he is lovely! And you should have invited him for breakfast!"

My family were friendly to Paul. We all chatted a bit before the service started. The service seemed very long. I was very self-conscious.

Afterwards, we all said our goodbyes. I had to head home to change and then head to work. Now I regretted that I hadn't organised to have lunch with Paul. Maybe I should have invited him for breakfast.

Romance Blossoms

With Paul's return to Wellington, our letter writing resumed. I took great delight in the arrival of his letters and would dance a little jig while heading up the driveway after checking the letter box. I read and re-read his letters. In fact, I pretty much memorised them. However, I remained cautious in my letters to him, being careful about what I shared.

A few weeks after Paul's visit, Simon and I were in the car together, driving somewhere. Out of the blue, Simon said, "I think that you should marry that Paul."

"Do you, now?"

"Yes. I think he would be really good for you."

"I'll bear that in mind."

"No, you won't!"

"No, I probably won't!"

The next time Paul and I met up, we met in Wellington. I stayed a weekend with Romy and Glenn and their girls (at this stage, the couple had two lovely little girls, Ashley and Lydia). On Sunday morning, I went to church with them and then went into Wellington by train to meet Paul.

Paul met me at the station. It was a lovely, sunny day, so we took a picnic lunch from the bakery into the botanic gardens and enjoyed a lovely afternoon together. We did a lot of hiking up and down hills.

We were both more relaxed this time. Our conversation flowed more easily, although there were still moments of quiet. Paul did not seem to be bothered about the quiet, so I decided to relax about it.

Of course, when I returned to Romy's, there was much discussion about this man. I told her that I liked him and thought he was a good friend. I explained just how quiet he was. Romy was keen to know how much I liked him and where our relationship was heading. I fudged my answers. In all honesty, I didn't know the answers.

The conversation with Romy did make me realise that I was viewing Paul differently. I was softening in my attitude towards him. I knew that I liked him. He was interesting and clever. I enjoyed his company. My respect for him was growing. I returned home and looked forward to his next letter.

I loved Paul's letters, but I must say they presented me with a challenge. He asked questions about my thoughts, my opinions, and my faith. As time went on, those questions took on a new intensity. He was frequently direct in what he asked. It was a relief when his questions were easier! He was persistent in wanting to know me better and was determined to form a friendship with me.

We made attempts to meet up together, but it took a few months before we managed to be in the same city again. Paul was heading to Australia for a month-long holiday and had arranged to stay for a couple of nights in Christchurch on his way to Australia.

Simon and Deb offered a room at their place. Paul leapt at the opportunity. He later admitted that he hoped to glean more information about me from them!

I organised to be off duty for the days when Paul was in Christchurch, as I was determined to make the most of our time together.

On the first full day, Paul and I drove to Akaroa. It was a beautifully sunny day in the middle of the week, so the scenic setting of Akaroa was shining in all of its brilliance. Also, it was quiet.

Paul and I engaged in some conversation on the way, but there were moments of quiet. I was less bothered by the quiet, but I must say that my head was working overtime. Seeing Paul again had made me realise two things:

1. I really liked this man and wondered if we would have a future together.
2. If there was to be a future for us, then I had to tell him my history.

The thought of telling Paul that I had been sexually abused as a child made me feel ill. Every time the car went quiet, I prayed. I prayed for wisdom and for courage. I prayed that I would find the right moment.

It was a lovely day. I really enjoyed Paul's company. We took some lovely walks and enjoyed a picnic lunch together. About lunchtime, I decided that I would wait until later to tell him about my history. For now, I would enjoy the time in Akaroa. With the decision made, I relaxed. But then I realised something. When walking around Akaroa, I wanted Paul to hold my hand. That could mean only one thing: I was falling for him.

Mid afternoon, we returned to Christchurch, where we were to have a meal with Simon and Debbie before we all headed out for a movie. Paul and I went straight to their place to wait for them to return from work.

As we sat in their lounge, I knew that this was the moment when I had to reveal my history. I took a big breath and then began.

I quietly and calmly explained in broad terms what had happened to me as a child and where it had led me. I talked about having committed myself to counselling and doing the work needed to find healing in my life. I talked about having been in a really dark place, saying that God had moved me through to this point. I said that I thought that although I had history and baggage, I was now healthy and ready to move on with my life.

Paul sat very quietly throughout and listened intently. When I finished, I sat quietly. My heart was racing. I was praying, "Please, Lord, let it be alright."

Paul lent forward, looked me in the eye, and said quietly and carefully, "Thank you for telling me. It hasn't come as a complete surprise. In your letters, there were hints that there was something. I do need to think about things."

It was a calm and careful response, which meant very much to me. I understood his need to process what I had shared. At the same time, I was desperate for reassurance.

Things might have been awkward between us at this moment, but they weren't really. Simon and Debbie arrived home shortly afterwards. I think that Paul and I both appreciated their company at that point. Their conversation was light and a welcome distraction.

After dinner, we all headed to the movies, with Simon driving. On arrival, I decided to be very brave. I quietly asked Paul if I could hold his hand. He smiled and took my hand in his. I had not expected it to feel so good! We held hands throughout the movie and in the back of the car on the way home. Part of me wanted to ask him what he was thinking, whereas part of me didn't want to know. That evening, I had given him my heart as well as my hand. I knew that I might well be headed for heartbreak.

I slept badly that night. My head replayed the day over and over again – all the conversations and the hand-holding. I wondered what the new day would bring. I was pleased to start the new day. I ate little for breakfast and then made my way to Simon and Debbie's place.

On my arrival, I was pleased (and relieved) to find Paul friendly and pleased to see me. There was no mention of our conversation of the previous day and I felt that it was appropriate to leave it to Paul to process the conversation and to initiate the next one to arise on the subject, but make no mistake, however: I was in agony.

Paul and I were to spend the morning together before I would take him to the airport for his flight out to Australia. The day was much cooler than the previous one. It took some time for the frost on the ground to clear. It was, however, dry, so we wrapped up in warm clothes and headed into town to spend some time looking around the arts centre and enjoying a lovely stroll around the Botanical Gardens. Walking hand in hand with him gave me some comfort, but our conversation was kept light.

All too soon, it was time to head to the airport. It was such a wrench preparing to say goodbye. We were both a little flustered. As we said goodbye, I looked up at Paul and asked, "Are we going to be alright?"

"I don't know, Suzanne. I need some time to think and to pray. OK?"

"OK, but …"

And so he left.

I cried all the way to work, later composing myself while I changed into uniform. I was quieter and more withdrawn than usual during my shift. Then I cried all the way home.

I knew that I had delivered a bombshell and was very concerned that I had scared Paul off. There was no way of getting in touch with him for the next month. I just had to wait for him to get in touch with me.

There was a long wait and the longer that I waited, the more pessimistic I became. I kept myself busy with work and study, but thoughts of Paul were never far from my mind.

Then a letter arrived. I recognised the writing straightaway. Usually, I would tear the envelope open and start reading the contents on my way inside the house. Not this time. I walked slowly inside, found a seat, and, with a big sigh, opened the envelope.

It was a lovely letter written while Paul was in Melbourne (his first stop). He explained that what I had shared with him earlier was not a complete shock. He wrote that there had been a few comments pointing to something in my letters and that my openness had brought them all together. He needed to give some thought to what had happened to me and also to how I was doing at this point. Had I worked through things to a healthy point? He explained that after taking time to think, to pray, and to read, he was of the opinion that I had reached a healthy point in my life. He commended me on my commitment to personal growth.

At this point, I could breathe again.

The letter contained more about his holiday thus far. I was so relieved that he was still writing to me! I sat and cried. I thanked God that not only was there great progress in my own life but also that Paul had been able to see it.

I wrote and wrote to Paul while he was away. I sent one long letter and then started another, to which I kept adding to, over the rest of the time. It was quite an epistle by the time I sent it. I was ready for his return.

There was even greater excitement when Paul rang me from Australia. I was so overwhelmed and found it hard to string sentences together. For the first time, Paul took the lead in drawing out the conversation. Just to hear his voice was amazing.

A week later, he called again. I better managed to keep my composure this time. Of all the romantic gestures that he could have made, there could have been nothing else that would have touched my heart as much.

I could now see very clearly that I had fallen in love with Paul. More than that, I had told him the worst and he hadn't run away. In that month, I realised how much I wanted him in my life. I was now suspicious that we would be spending our lives together.

While Paul was still away, I applied for a week's holiday to be taken a couple of months later. It seemed like an eternity away, but it was the soonest that I could get leave. I booked flights and prayed that there would be an opportunity to meet up with Paul before then.

Engagement and Wedding

On Paul's return to Wellington, we made phone calls and sent letters to each other. We did manage to find a weekend when I was not working and when Paul was free. He suggested that we could meet up in Picton for the weekend. He would come across on the ferry, and I would drive up from Christchurch. It was a great suggestion and, one that meant we would be together even sooner.

I booked into a bed and breakfast for the weekend. Paul later asked where I was staying. He booked a room there also.

It was quite a drive from Christchurch to Picton. I was excited to see Paul again. The trip was pleasant enough on a fine winter's day.

I arrived before Paul did and I checked into the bed and breakfast. There was time for me to look around Picton a little before his ferry came in. I was at the wharf well ahead of time, just in case the ferry made good time. It didn't! When the ferry arrived, I was very excited to see Paul walk off. He greeted me with a large smile and a big hug. It seemed he was also pleased to see me!

We took Paul's things through to the bed and breakfast. The host, seeing us walk into the foyer hand in hand, offered us a shared room to keep our costs down. With much blushing on my part, we politely declined.

We headed to the local pizzeria for a meal. I must say that I had no appetite at all.

The following morning greeted us with a hard frost and with fog covering the harbour. Not to be deterred, we collected lunch from a local bakery and then headed out on a walk down the length of the peninsula. It was incredibly good to be together. We talked about all manner of things. We asked each other all sorts of questions, the "What do you think about …?" sort of questions. I remember a moment when Paul made the point that it was important to consider whether the other person would be a good wife (or husband) and a good mother (or father). In the context of our questions and general discussion, I noted the comment as an interesting one to consider.

We walked and talked for about an hour and a half. The fog remained as the temperature stayed very cold. We came across a flattened area that had a bench seat which seemed to be positioned to admire the view. We laughed and said that the view of the fog was lovely. Paul gestured that it would be good to sit for a few moments. We sat and held hands.

Paul turned towards me and said, "I have another question for you."

"Aha."

"Suzanne, will you marry me?"

"Oh, I don't know."

"Oh."

"I mean, where did that come from? I mean, I need to think. Can I think about it?"

"Of course you can!"

My heart raced and my mind went into overdrive. For the first time ever, Paul just quietly talked. For the life of me, I can't remember what he talked about! I was having my own conversation in my head.

I knew that I loved this man, but I also knew that I must be completely sure before I agreed to marry him. I knew it would be completely cruel to say yes now and then change my mind later. I prayed. I looked at him. I knew that he would be an excellent husband to me. He would also be a great dad. There was no doubt of that, and there was no doubt in my mind that he loved me. I said another prayer and took a big breath.

"Paul, could you ask me again now?"

"Certainly. Suzanne, will you marry me?"

"Yes, Paul, yes. I will marry you!"

"Yes?"

"Yes!"

"Are you sure?"

"Oh yes!"

"Oh, wow!"

At this point, the fog lifted! The view was stunning. We took a few moments to enjoy it before we continued on our walk. At the end of the peninsula, we sat and enjoyed our picnic. We struggled to keep our eyes off each other. There was an awful lot of giggling as well.

Paul apologised that he had no engagement ring. He thought that if I was going to wear a ring, then I should help to choose it. I told him that a plastic one would be just fine. He laughed and said that he thought we could do better than that.

On our return walk, our minds turned to more practical matters, like when and where we would be married. We knew we also faced a decision about where we would live. It was a conversation about hopes and dreams, but it was more about love than anything.

On our return to Picton, we phoned my parents to let them know. They were not even a little surprised. I later commented that they could have at least pretended to be surprised!

Later that day, my fiancé and I walked into Picton to have dinner. On the way into town, Paul stopped me and asked me what I thought of kissing now that we are engaged. I smiled and said that I thought it might be a nice option now. So there and then we had our first kiss. It was not particularly good in terms of technique, but, then again, I had never kissed a man before and Paul had never kissed a lady before. I loved it! To be held very close and to taste his lips ... I was happy to practise more!

Of course, the more that I fell for Paul, the more difficult saying goodbye to him became. The one thought that made this particular separation more bearable was that I would be in Wellington for a whole week in just a few weeks' time. Of course there would be letters and phone calls in the meantime.

Paul returned to Wellington with a massive smile on his face to announce that he was engaged, when few people knew he was dating me, and none of them had met me.

I returned to Christchurch to find myself tremendously ribbed about my mystery man. My family were happy for me. There was the excitement of an anticipated wedding. However, I think we were all aware that Paul and I would need to decide about where we would live. My dad helpfully suggested that Paul could commute to work from Christchurch during the week! We were just so keen to be together.

My next visit to Wellington was so special. Spending a whole week together in the same city meant that Paul and I could have lots more time together. We saw each other as much as we could, scheduling our meeting up around Paul's work. On my first day in Wellington, Paul took me shopping for an engagement ring. I was nervous, whereas Paul was excited. We headed down to Lambton Quay and discovered just how many jewellery shops there were.

It was a disaster almost immediately. We had made a big mistake by failing to have a very simple discussion beforehand. We did not talk about the cost of rings or what we (or, more correctly, he) would be spending. In the first jeweller's shop, I was looking at the very inexpensive rings while he was looking at the most expensive! I couldn't believe it. He had me trying on all sorts of rings. I was getting more and more anxious about the cost.

Eventually, I managed to bundle Paul out of the shop and get him out onto the street. I told him he couldn't possibly spend that kind of money on a ring. He informed me that he could. We had a bit of discussion. In the end, we reached a compromise. I would try on rings and look to find what I liked and what suited me. He would worry about the price.

Into the next jeweller's shop we went. Paul politely explained to the jeweller that we wanted to look at engagement rings, saying that his fiancée did not want to know the prices. The jeweller smiled and asked Paul where we would like to start.

Eventually, we chose a beautiful ring with three diamonds. At the time, I did not know what Paul paid for it. It was some years before I learnt the price. He was generous in his gift to me and it has been worn since with great pride, seeing that it represented that this amazing man loved me and had chosen to marry me.

This time in Wellington, Paul took me on a grand tour to meet his family. On a Saturday, I met his sister and his brothers. On a Sunday, he took me to church and then to meet his mother. I was very nervous, but I was also intrigued about meeting his family. Paul was a little nervous about introducing me to his mum, but it went well.

Of course, I introduced Paul to Romy, Glenn, and their girls. I was nervous about it, but it went well.

The time came for me and Paul to start having some of the more serious conversations. Bit by bit, we made our way through the decisions to be made. We decided that with my job, it would be easier for me to relocate to Wellington. It was a hard decision for me – in fact, it was the only difficult decision I made during this time. I would sell my house in Christchurch ahead of the wedding. My parents said that I was welcome to return home for the intervening time. At the time, I was undertaking some study. After much discussion, Paul and I settled on having our wedding on Waitangi Day – February 6, 1998. It was a public holiday which, in that year, fell on a Friday, making the weekend a long one.

There were discussions about wedding details, but, by and large, decisions about the wedding were easy for me to make. Paul and I had our eyes firmly fixed on the bigger picture. We knew that we were preparing for a married life together. This helped to keep our wedding in perspective. In fact, we spent more time reading books about marriage and discussing them than we spent doing anything else related to the wedding.

Don and Ruth offered us a course in marriage preparation. We jumped at the opportunity. The course provided us with the prompts to talk through other points or issues that we hadn't already covered.

Despite living in different cities, we managed to fit in time with Don and Ruth, scheduling it for the times when Paul was in Christchurch.

In the next few months, Paul and I sent letters to each other, had very long phone calls with each other, and made a large number of visits to see each other, whether in Wellington or Christchurch.

One afternoon while Paul was in Christchurch, he and I had a conversation about soul mates and about whether there was more than one person who was right for any one individual. There was some chat, and Paul expressed his opinion (as a mathematician) that there must be more than one person that you could meet and then marry. His point being that, statistically speaking, the possibility of meeting *the* right person was very slim. I looked across at him and explained that I didn't think that such was the case. Paul started to explain the chances of meeting one person amongst six billion. Quickly, I jumped in and explained what I meant. For me, Paul was a gift from God himself. To me, it was obvious that God knew me and knew what I needed. I told Paul that I thought that God had picked the very best for me. Not only had he picked the best, but he had also found a way for Paul and me to get to know each other in a way that was safe for me. It was also an effective way, as it happened. Paul sat and looked at me very quietly. He remained quiet for a few moments as he thought about what I had said. He asked me whether I really thought that. Oh yes, I did.

During this time, with the prospect of marriage, I worried that I would have flashbacks and experience an exacerbation of my nightmares. During our engagement, I had just a few flashbacks. It was always distressing for me. To Paul's credit, he coped remarkably well. When I had a flashback, he would hold me gently and talk very calmly, usually praying. At one point, I was concerned enough to ring Peter to talk the matter through. Peter's first response was to tease me about what Paul and I were up to. But then he was reassuring and told me that we were reacting in the right way. He believed my problem would settle quickly, which it did.

I was, however, now faced with a new problem. It was one that I had never even considered. I was madly in love with Paul. I felt safe with him and enjoyed his company very much. Now I fancied him! Early on in our engagement, we agreed that there were some things that were best left until we were married. It was a good decision. It was the right decision. At times, it was just so difficult to stick with, though. I loved him so much, and I loved his touch. At times, it was agonising for me to restrain myself. After all, we were going to be married soon. We had, however, agreed on where the line must lie. We also realised that the closer to that line we allowed ourselves to get, the harder it became not to cross it.

It felt so wonderful to love Paul and to know that he loved me. I trusted him without reserve. What might have been a difficult time was simply magical.

Paul's love had a dramatic effect on me. His eyes would light up when he saw me. His delight in spending time with me led to a dramatic increase in my self-confidence. I became surer of myself. For many years, I had hated my body. Fundamentally, my body had made me vulnerable for so long that I felt dirty, but now even that was changing. I didn't transform into a gorgeous supermodel, but I moved closer to being comfortable with myself.

Finally, the week of our wedding arrived. Paul and his family arrived in Christchurch. More guests arrived. There was a buzz in the air.

I awoke on the morning of the wedding to find fog! This was something of a surprise. It was a reminder of another foggy morning, though. I met Romy, Debbie, and Ashley at the hairdresser's. I felt very calm and very happy. Time seemed to drag! We emerged late in the morning with our hair and make-up complete. Having entered the hairdresser's shop amidst the fog, we found upon our exit a warm summer's day with beautiful blue skies.

On returning to Mum and Dad's, I detected a growing nervousness amongst the group. I managed to remain calm. Mum was insistent that we should all have something to eat, but food was of no interest to me at all. I managed to eat a sandwich. Everyone was happy about that.

About midday, I changed into my wedding dress. It was so lovely, it felt soft and romantic. Just putting the dress on made me smile.

The service was due to start at 1 p.m. I was keen to get to the church. There was some banter with my driver, who told me that the bride should arrive a few moments late in order to allow the guests to arrive and take their seats. I did point out that anyone who knew me would know that I was never late.

Finally, I and my wedding party were allowed to leave Mum and Dad's house. I think this was permitted in order to placate me. I noted that the driver took the long route and drove slowly! The car, with its air conditioning, was a pleasant place to be, as the temperature outside was well over thirty degrees Celsius.

The one part of the day that I dreaded was walking into the church and having everyone turn to look at me. So now, as I stood in the foyer of the church, I was a little nervous. My nervous giggle gave me away.

The music started. My bridesmaids walked down to the front of the church. My dad took my arm. He asked me, "You sure?"

"Oh yes!"

"Well, let's go, then."

As Dad and I walked across the back of the church, all eyes turned to look at me. I could feel the blood rush to my face. Then Dad led me around to walk down the aisle. I could see Paul waiting for me at the front of the church. When he smiled, I relaxed. All the planning, all the letters, all the phone calls, and all the visits had led to this moment. I took Paul's hand to hold. All at once, I realised just how nervous he was. I smiled and squeezed his hand.

The service was wonderful. It was simple and very personal. It felt amazing to be amongst our family and friends in the church where Paul had met me months earlier.

Paul and I knew there would be a significant number of non-Christians in the church that day, so we had given Don a free hand in terms of what he could say. He spoke very powerfully about love and commitment. There was, of course, a little light teasing of the bride and groom.

Paul and I turned to say our vows to each other. He went first, and I followed. We had chosen fairly conservative vows, having decided to use words significant to us so that we could memorise them. Paul spoke his vows to me so clearly and with such commitment that I got teary-eyed.

I looked up into his blue eyes to say my vows to him. Incredible happiness was written all over his face. I knew these words, and I meant every one of them. Halfway through saying my vows, I had to stop, as my emotions bubbled up and I wanted to cry. Don prompted me. I nodded. I smiled at Paul, who squeezed my hand. I swallowed hard, took a big breath, and completed my vows.

After that, Paul and I exchanged rings and were invited to kiss ...

All too soon, the service was over. We stayed at church to have afternoon tea with all our guests. It really was great to have a few moments with our friends. There was a wedding cake to cut. We escaped delivering any speeches at this point.

I was desperate for just a few moments with Paul on our own, so we retreated into the church, which was now mostly empty. We enjoyed a few moments to check in with each other.

Between the afternoon tea and the reception, Paul, I, and the bridal party moved off to have photos taken. The reception was held on the tenth floor of an inner-city hotel with stunning views of Christchurch. It was a lovely evening. I found it truly wonderful to spend time with everyone.

My dad's speech was complimentary to both Paul and me. He had made it very clear that the tone of people's speeches was to be complimentary and kind. We offered the opportunity for anyone else to speak. It was lovely to hear many kind words of encouragement.

Over the course of the evening, I became a little more nervous. The day had been truly amazing and very special. Soon, it would be just the two of us. I was a little nervous about how things would be and how I might react. I think Paul realised that I was getting nervous, so he suggested that it might be a good time for us to slip away.

We sought out close family and members of the bridal party to say farewell before trying unsuccessfully to quietly slip out the door.

It had been a long and very hot day. It had been the wonderful day that we had imagined and more. But for both of us, it had been all rather tiring. It was bliss to be alone.

So here we were, both of us tired. I was nervous. Paul knew it. When he looked at me, his hesitancy showed on his face. I smiled. He smiled. I leant in to kiss him. He said, "We don't have to if …". I pulled him closer to kiss him again.

Suffice it to say that we enjoyed the first night of our honeymoon.

Paul and I had set aside two weeks to celebrate the start of our married life. I had left all of the honeymoon arrangements to him. He had organised an amazing place for us to stay in Queenstown.

Queenstown is a beautiful scenic spot. For us now, arriving in late summer, it was just lovely. We enjoyed taking walks in the area, but most of all we enjoyed each other's company and being married.

In the last days of our time in Queenstown, Paul was keen to introduce me to off-road biking in a very gentle way. It sounded like a great idea. We walked into Queenstown to hire bikes. It was already warm. We decided to bike the track from Queenstown to Frankton and back, with a stop for lunch at Frankton. It was just 6 km each way. This was no problem, not even for me!

Halfway through the ride, I felt a little unwell. I put it down to the heat. Maybe I was a little dehydrated. I didn't think too much of it.

Following our ride, we went to find cold drinks and air conditioning. At this point, I realised that I really didn't feel well. I mentioned to Paul that I was feeling off colour, saying that maybe it was because of the heat of the day. As I mentioned this to Paul, it crossed my mind that I might be pregnant.

At the end of our honeymoon, we reluctantly returned to real life. For us, this meant returning to Christchurch to pack my car and then drive to Wellington together. I made heart-wrenching goodbyes to my family. Just outside of Christchurch, Paul and I stopped for a drink, at which time I had a really good cry.

A New City Is Home

Arriving in Wellington Harbour on the ferry, I found the view simply stunning. It was a still, clear night. The lights of the city sparkled and reflected off the water. It was great to finally arrive, but I was tired from the driving and the emotion of the day. I felt unwell, which I blamed on the motion of the boat.

Now I looked out over Wellington Harbour and felt very little. I was rather dwarfed by the task of settling into a new city.

Paul held me close as the boat docked. I found great comfort from being in his arms.

It was midnight by the time we drove off the ferry and made our way to our flat in Island Bay.

The first weeks in our new home were busy. We left some boxes packed as we looked forward to hunting for a more permanent home.

It was organised that I would start my new job at Wellington Women's Hospital a full week later. The first few days I spent at orientation, which included extensive training about emergency procedures, with a very strong emphasis on earthquakes. I wondered what on earth I was doing in Wellington!

I was to work in the Neonatal Intensive Care Unit. Mostly, the staff were welcoming, although there was a small group of staff who liked to test and harass any new staff members, especially those who had worked in a NICU elsewhere. I kept my head down and tried to adjust to the different ways of doing things. I must admit that a lot of my co-workers' behaviour just washed off me. After all, I was madly in love with my new husband. Each day, I went home to an amazing man.

During my first week of work, I continued to feel unwell intermittently. By now, I was overdue for my period. I pondered how soon I could take a pregnancy test. By the following Friday evening, I realised that I showed enough indications of being pregnant that it was worth it to me to buy a pregnancy test. Paul and I made a trip to an after-hours pharmacy to buy an at-home pregnancy test.

The next morning, I awoke early and felt rather seedy. Paul was still asleep. I lay in bed needing to go to the toilet, but not wanting to disturb Paul. I was also trying to decide whether or not I would take the test.

I became sufficiently uncomfortable, so I quietly made my way out of bed and walked to the other end of the flat. I went into the bathroom.

A few moments later, I looked at the positive indication on the test strip. I didn't know whether to laugh or cry. I was stunned.

How could I be pregnant already? Of course, I understood *how*, but nonetheless I was stunned. A number of my friends struggled with infertility. I had just assumed that it would take time for me to become pregnant.

After a few more minutes in the bathroom, I headed back to bed to find Paul sat bolt upright in bed, with an expectant look on his face. "Well?"

"What do you mean?"

"Did you do the test?"

"Yes."

"And?"

I handed him the result. He looked at me rather blankly.

"The two lines mean that I am pregnant."

"Wow! Are you sure?"

"Oh yes!"

"You can't be very …"

"Well, Paul!"

"Wow!"

We sat cuddled up in bed, giggling like teenagers. We were so excited and very pleased. Later on, we made a phone call to my parents to share the news. Needless to say, they were thrilled. We visited Paul's mum a little later to share the news with her.

Then we agreed that we would not tell anyone else, just in case I miscarried. It was a pointless decision, as I had significant morning sickness and people were able to join the dots all too easily.

Three months later, Paul and I moved into our own home and started to get ready for our baby.

My morning sickness was such that I had to reduce my hours at work but even that was a struggle for me, though.

Just over a month before our due date, Paul and I made the trip to Christchurch to visit family. Simon and Debbie had welcomed their first daughter, Isabella Grace, into their lives. We were eager to meet her.

A week after our return to Wellington, our baby was born on a Sunday evening. A precious little girl. I will forever remember the look of absolute joy on Paul's face. Our daughter was born just over three weeks early. She was little – 2,980 gm – with just a little bit of red hair. We named her Abigail Zoe. *Abigail* means "father's joy", and *Zoe* means "life".

Later that night when Paul had returned home, I was looking at Abigail and thanking God for her. I remember a wave of fear suddenly washing over me. Very quickly, I prayed: "God, you have given me a beautiful daughter, but I am scared. I wonder how I can keep her safe. How do I protect her from the world?"

I watched Abigail quietly breathing. Suddenly, there was incredible calm and peace in the room. I held her close and prayed again. "Lord, I know that she is yours and that you have allowed us this incredible privilege to parent her. Lord, she is yours. I place her firmly in your hands."

Family Life Begins

The first year of Abigail's life was full of challenges. She was little and quickly became jaundiced, which made her even more reluctant to feed or even to awake. Paul and I had major feeding issues with her. We faced the very real possibility of having to admit her to NICU because she was dehydrated. We resorted to feeding her breast milk via a bottle for a number of weeks until I was able to persuade her to breastfeed again. This meant that I was up to feed her twice a night for two months. Each feed would have me up for an hour and a half. It was very tiring!

Despite my very best care, Abigail remained slow to gain weight. There were mutterings from the GP and Plunket nurse about that. Yet she hit every other milestone, either on schedule or ahead of it.

On top of that, Abigail had reflux and was very uncomfortable with it. Both she and I shed many tears.

During this year, I was homesick for Christchurch and for the company and support of my family – in particular, for the support of my parents. The situation became more acute when my dad was diagnosed with cancer of the tongue, which required surgery to remove the cancer and a significant part of his tongue. I was keen to make my way back to Christchurch, but at that point Abby was very little and struggling. Paul and my parents persuaded me that it would be better for me to remain in Wellington and to focus on

Abby. There were dozens of phone calls back and forth. The news from Christchurch was positive. Although I found it difficult to be away, I was reassured by these progress reports.

As Abigail hit six months of age, things started improving. They kept getting better until she was about ten months of age. Then we struggled with ear infection after ear infection. We seemed to be living at the doctor's surgery.

Just after Abigail turned a year old, I started to feel unwell. A positive pregnancy test confirmed my and Paul's suspicions. We were over the moon. Unfortunately, just a few weeks later I had a miscarriage. I was devastated. Paul was very kind and supportive, which did help.

One Monday morning when Abigail was about fifteen months old, she awoke covered in a rash. Off to the doctor's we went. This time we saw a locum.

The locum declared Abigail's rash to be viral. He said that it would clear in a few days. Then he decided to check her ears and throat while we were there.

Sure enough, the locum announced that my daughter had an ear infection that would require antibiotics. He commented that she did seem to have had a number of ear infections lately.

Next, he looked into her mouth and asked me, "Have they decided to leave her cleft palate, or are they going to repair it?"

My heart skipped a beat. A massive penny had dropped!

"What cleft palate?" I asked. The locum went very pale as his mouth dropped open. "Oh, please keep talking. It all makes sense."

He explained that Abigail had a small cleft, or hole, in her posterior soft palate. Sometimes, when it is very small it could be left alone. I was informed that Abigail might need orthodontic work once she hit her teens.

Wow! I cried all the way home. Everything made sense now. I felt such guilt that I hadn't picked up on the cleft palate, but then I remembered that a number of doctors, paediatricians, and Plunket nurses had seen my daughter and had failed to recognise her cleft palate.

I made a frantic phone call to Paul at work. He was surprised by the news, but he remained very calm. I appreciated his calmness, as I felt my world crumbling around me.

Later on of course, I had conversations about Abigail's cleft palate with my family and friends, complete with a number of "Oh, of course" reactions from them.

Paul and I put our heads together to talk about what to do next. We made an appointment to see our family doctor the following week. We turned up together – a united front.

It was immediately clear that our doctor had not had an update, so I said, "I brought Abby in last week, as she had a rash. But while we were there, the locum doctor found a cleft palate. The rash is gone, but not the cleft palate."

The doctor went pale. Her mouth dropped. "No," she said.

"Yes."

The doctor, managed to entice Abigail to open her mouth, and clearly sighted what had been missed for so long. "Oh no," she said.

She recovered quickly and gave Paul and me the same explanation as I had received the previous week. But we were ready for it this time.

I said, "Having heard all of that, we, under the circumstances, would like Abigail to be referred on to whoever she should be referred to for a second opinion."

The doctor was not convinced, so Paul reiterated what I had said. The doctor then told us that she would send a referral to the Plastic Surgery Department at Hutt Hospital. She warned us there would be a wait, as these places usually had long waiting lists.

Forty-eight hours later, I received a phone call from Hutt Hospital to inform me of an appointment time. The doctors were keen to see Abigail very quickly. The receptionist was concerned that if she simply posted the letter with the appointment time, it would arrive too late.

So we had seen the doctor on the Monday, had been phoned on the Wednesday, and were to present at the hospital on the Friday.

Friday saw us make the trip to Hutt Hospital. Arriving with time to spare we made our way into the hospital to find the clinic. It turned out that we were being seen in the pre-admitting clinic simply because that was where they could squeeze us in. Paul and I were tense, which Abigail quickly picked up on. She clung tight to me.

The Surgeon invited us through to an examination room. It was a small clinical room with a basket of toys in one corner. We all took seats. Abigail kept clinging tightly to me. The surgeon was a lovely Malaysian man. He was a real gentleman – very kind and very quietly spoken.

The surgeon asked Paul and me a long list of questions – about our family histories, my pregnancy, Abigail's feeding history, her weight gain, her ear infections, her speech, and even how she vomited!

Then the surgeon sat back in his seat, put his pen down, and looked at us. "Well, Abigail has a cleft palate that will need to be repaired. She will need surgery."

I sat stunned. I looked at him. "Oh. You could look in her mouth before you make the decision," I said.

"I could if it will help you, but your answers have given me all the information that I need."

I wanted to run, but I couldn't move. I held Abigail close as tears made their way down my face.

In all honesty, the surgeon was lovely with us. He talked about the long-term effects on Abigail's speech if her cleft palate was not corrected. He explained that this type of repair is normally done when a child is nine months to ten months old, so Abigail's was considered a late repair. He even apologised that her cleft palate had been missed for so long.

He described the surgery and the post-operative care that Abigail would need. He explained that she would have auditory grommets inserted at the same time. Children with cleft palates often have narrow Eustachian tubes and, therefore, suffer frequent ear infections.

Then the surgeon told us the date of the surgery – less than two weeks away. I was stunned. A gasp escaped my mouth. "Do we get time to think about this?" I asked.

"No. This has to be done. I am sorry, but she must have this surgery – and very soon. There is no decision to be made."

I looked across at Paul, who managed a weak smile and nodded his head. I closed my eyes and leant forward to slowly kiss my daughter on the top of her head. I looked up to find both men looking at me. I managed a nod of my head.

"Well done."

We left the hospital and went out into a beautiful, sunny day. It seemed wrong. My heart was hurting, so I thought it should be rainy and stormy outside. All the way home, questions went around and around my head: "Why, God? Why this? Why Abigail?"

Later that day, I prayed (or, rather, I unloaded all my feelings) to him. I told God that I didn't understand why my daughter had a cleft palate. I told him that I didn't know if I had the strength to walk along the path that was ahead of me. I told him that this demanded strength and courage, and I said that I had none of either. I begged him to heal Abigail so there would be no need for surgery.

That night, I cried myself to sleep as Paul cradled me in his arms. I think that I understood what this surgery was going to be like, whereas Paul understood that it really was the best thing for our daughter.

Falling asleep that night, I knew I wanted a miracle. And I knew that I was going to need Paul if I was to be able to walk this path.

A few days later, I arranged to change to a different Medical Practice and a different GP. I also rang to change to a different Plunket Rooms. I wanted to be able to trust the health professionals in our lives. It seemed time to make these changes.

A Bumpy Journey

The day of surgery loomed. My mum would be up from Christchurch that week to visit, which seemed providential.

Three days before her surgery, Abigail came down with a cold. She was miserable. The day before surgery, I rang the hospital to see if the surgery would go ahead. I was assured that, yes, it would. I was told that Paul and I should present as planned.

At 5:30 the next morning, we all stumbled from our beds. Abby was allowed some small sips of water, but it was to be nil by mouth from 6 a.m. onwards. Our anxiety levels being what they were, we all took nil by mouth that morning!

It was still dark as we rode the forty minutes to Hutt Hospital. All the way, I had a nagging thought that the surgery would not happen.

On arrival, we waited for Abby to be admitted. The nurse was busy and distracted. Abigail was feeling unwell, as her temperature was elevated. And I, well, I was a little grumpy.

The nurse handed me a gown to put on Abby. I looked at the nurse and asked if she would check that the surgeon would be operating on Abby, given that she was unwell. The nurse looked at me like I must be crazy, but she did go to ask.

The nurse was away for about ten minutes. Once she returned, she said, "I have the anaesthetist on the phone. He wants to know if Abigail has been eating and drinking alright. She has, hasn't she?"

I explained that my daughter had indeed had a loss of appetite. The nurse left to talk to the anaesthetist on the phone.

She returned quickly this time and informed me and Paul that the surgery would have to be postponed. I was upset, but I bit my tongue. Then she commented that it was a shame that I hadn't rung on the previous day to check.

"Actually, I did, and I was told to bring her this morning. The poor kid has been dragged from her bed and brought all the way here unnecessarily."

The nurse was embarrassed and didn't know quite what to say. Then she asked if Paul and I would like some toast for Abigail before we returned home.

Poor Abby whimpered in my arms. She was miserable and rather bewildered about where she was.

A doctor stepped into the room at this point. He set about explaining why the surgery couldn't happen. I looked him in the eyes and quietly said, "My frustration is not that the surgery is cancelled. I understand that. It would have been better to avoid bringing my daughter out like this when she is so unwell. I did try to avoid this by ringing in yesterday." He was apologetic and said that someone would be in touch about the new date for the surgery.

Paul and I called into Lower Hutt for some breakfast on the way home. We all needed to have something in our stomachs. Plus, we hoped to avoid getting caught in the rush-hour traffic.

It was a very quiet ride home in the car.

Abby's surgery was rescheduled for a few weeks later. Mum had returned home. In the meantime, Paul and I had the opportunity to talk about the stress and how we could better cope with it. We were now much clearer about how we would need to support each other. We knew ways to do so.

We also made use of the time to seek prayer for Abigail and, indeed, for her parents!

Our return to Hutt Hospital a few weeks later was another very early start on a cold morning. The trip could not have been more different from the previous one. Abby was well. There was a sense of peace in the middle of the stressful situation.

Even the way we were greeted as we entered the ward was much different, as the staff nurse and the registrar quickly checked in with Paul and me, enquiring after Abigail's health. Their relief was evident when we reassured them that she was well. She was bumped up on the list, which meant that our waiting time was significantly reduced.

It is incredibly difficult to present a child for any surgery, but when you arrive with a well child, knowing that she will be spending the night in the Intensive Care Unit because of the surgery, you feel absolute agony. I think that without Paul there to support me, I would have scooped Abigail up and headed for the door.

Paul and I waited quietly in the ward until we were summoned to take Abby to the theatre suite. I carried her in my arms as the nurse escorted us. Formalities were completed and Abigail's details were checked.

The anaesthetist invited us into the preparation room. I knew that there was going to be no easy way of doing the next part of the process. I knew we were going to have to leave our daughter in the arms of strangers.

The anaesthetist told us that he would place a mask on Abby's face. He warned us that she would not like it and was likely to protest. He explained that protesting was unpleasant but OK. Abby would take some big breaths and then quickly become sleepy from the gas. The team would wait till she was asleep, and then they would do what they needed to do before they rolled her trolley next door for the operation. Paul and I would need to leave once Abby was asleep.

While Abby was still in my arms, the mask was placed on her face. Sure enough, she resisted, but quite quickly she fell asleep. The anaesthetist lifted her gently and quickly from my arms and then placed her gently on the trolley. Paul and I kissed her on her forehead, and then we were ushered out.

My head knew that Abigail was in safe hands. I even understood that the surgery was necessary. Still, my heart was breaking. Staff suggested that Paul and I head to the hospital café for a cup of tea before heading back up to the ward to wait.

Time passed by very slowly. It seemed to take forever before we were finally informed that the surgery had been completed and that the recovery staff would appreciate it if we headed to the recovery area. No second invitation was required!

Paul and I arrived to find Abby very agitated. She was keen to be held by Mum, but she was restless. I felt very useless as I tried hard to soothe and calm her.

Shortly afterwards, we were all taken through to ICU. Because cleft-palate surgery is the type of surgery it is, it presents a risk of swelling or post-surgical bleeding, which might cause an occlusion to the airway. At Hutt Hospital, children who undergo surgery routinely spend their first night in the ICU, where their breathing is closely monitored.

The ICU staff were incredibly kind, reassuring, and informative. Although high-tech, the unit was small and quiet. Within a short time, Abigail started to settle. The staff had seated me in a large, comfortable chair. I nestled Abby against my body. We all started to relax.

A couple of hours later, staff suggested that Paul and I should head out for dinner. In fact, one staff nurse suggested that while we had babysitters handy, we should have a dinner date! Abby was settled to sleep in the cot.

Somewhat reluctantly, Paul and I headed away to find some food. As we left the hospital, we agreed that this hardly felt like a date. We were keen to be away for a short time only.

Unfortunately, our choice of doner kebabs was a terrible one. The following day, we would both be struck with a terrible case of food poisoning. This was not at all helpful in the circumstances.

On our return to ICU, we found Abigail just waking up. Together, Paul and I read with her and settled her back down for the night. Our plan was for Paul to return home overnight while I slept in the ward overnight. From there, I could be sent for if I was needed.

There was little sleep for me that night. After a couple of hours of fitful sleep, I headed back to the ICU to check on Abigail. It seemed that she was sleeping fitfully. For the rest of the night, I dozed on and off in the chair beside her cot. Abigail would awake and whimper, so I would awake and talk quietly to her while rubbing her back. When the next morning arrived, we were both exhausted.

We were pleased to see Paul return. As the morning went on, he and I became increasingly unwell. At one point in the mid morning, the medical staff arrived to review Abby's progress. They were very pleased with everything, so Paul and I were returned to the ward with instructions to encourage Abby to drink and start eating.

All went really well, so well, in fact, that Abby was discharged home two days earlier than had initially been indicated.

Abigail healed incredibly well. Time after time at her outpatient appointments, the reports were always much better than I had dared hope for. The cleft-palate repair is so very good that at times it is missed by dentists and doctors. She was referred for speech therapy but was discharged from it very quickly, as her speech was developing at the expected level for her age – or even better. Abby had no more ear infections. The grommets remained in place significantly longer than the six to twelve months we had initially hoped for.

A few months after Abby's surgery, I found myself to be pregnant again. Paul and I were both thrilled with the news, but this time I was somewhat nervous about being pregnant. For the first few months, I was nervous that I would have a miscarriage, not to mention the fact that I was now enjoying the ever present morning sickness.

At the end of May 2001, Paul and I welcomed a baby boy into our family. We named him Rory Paul. *Rory* means "a strong, red-headed leader". Indeed, like his older sister, Rory was born with red hair.

Epilogue

Time certainly does seem to fly by, especially when you are raising young children – and more so when you leave behind the disturbed nights' sleep of the first few years! My mother once commented that when children are old enough to be in school, the years just speed past. The rhythm of school terms and holidays, along with the ebb and flow of the seasons, does seem to give the feel of time racing past.

In our home now, Paul and I have two teenagers. This certainly makes it a very different season for us. The intervening years have, by and large, been great.

Paul and I made some significant changes during that time. Not long after Rory was born, Paul's manager gave approval for us to move to Christchurch to live. Paul officially worked as part of the Wellington team, but he was able to work from a distance, in Christchurch. I had been rather homesick in Wellington. We believed there would be some benefits in being closer to my family. There was always the understanding that we might have to return to live in Wellington at some point.

Just after Rory's first birthday, Paul and I sold our Wellington house and moved to Christchurch, the garden city. We spent a little time house-hunting without any success, so we decided to build a new home. We went in with our eyes open to the fact that it can be a stressful process, but for us it was a wonderful project.

Over time, as Abby and then Rory approached starting school at the age of five years, we applied (successfully) for places for them at Middleton Grange School. Attending school there had been such a positive experience for me. Paul and I were keen that it should be the same for Abby and Rory.

I spent some time working as a staff nurse part-time or on a casual basis. I experienced a constant juggling of work, home, study, and church commitments. Ultimately, Paul and I felt that the challenges of trying to fit things in around my shift work were proving difficult, so I stepped away from nursing. It was the right thing to do at that time. I had no real regrets. I have missed it at times, though.

It has been wonderful to watch our children grow as individuals and, in many ways, flourish. It has been great to watch them develop their own relationships with their grandparents. For Paul and me, it has been great to have my Mum and Dad's support and encouragement – all the while holding us accountable in our parenting!

During our years in Christchurch we, as a family have been committed to local church. Over the years we have been involved in home groups – even leading one for some time, and have been involved in so many other church-related activities. I think that each of us has found outlets for the gifts and skills that we have. To see them be used and extended is very exciting. I have particularly enjoyed being involved with a number of children through Sunday school programmes for children of different ages. I carry a real awareness that the foundation that others built into my life when I was very young was very important to me in those darker moments that arrived later in my life.

Paul, Abigail, Rory, and I have made great friends. All four of us have grown in our walk with God. We have all loved living in Christchurch, as it has offered us a lovely lifestyle. The South Island of New Zealand offers some truly beautiful scenery and an amazing array of activities to try. We have celebrated many wonderful family holidays in places around our beautiful island and farther afield.

In September 2010, life changed dramatically in Christchurch when we were woken early in the morning by an earthquake of 7.1 magnitude located to the west of Christchurch. It was a terrifying experience for all. Despite the intensity of the earthquake, there was no loss of life. Some people suffered minimal injuries, and some buildings and the city's infrastructure were damaged. Our family lost power, water, and the use of the phone line, but these were minor inconveniences. Of course, having lived in Wellington (the city in New Zealand expected to face a large earthquake), we were well organised and had emergency supplies. The city experienced regular aftershocks, but there was a real sense that we had gotten off very lightly and that all would be well.

February 22, 2011, changed all of that. A 6.3-magnitude earthquake struck at lunchtime. This time, it was much closer to the city. Although registering lower on the Richter scale, the earthquake was shallow and close. The city was shaken to its very core. This time, the damage was major, with falling masonry and collapsed buildings. There was the accompanying loss of 185 lives, and numerous people were injured. In addition, for us it was terrifying to find ourselves in different parts of the city, with the children at school and with Paul right in the middle of the Central Business District. Our relief was immense when we were once again all at home together.

My parents' home took significant damage. As they were closer to the epicentre, the trauma was huge for them.

The story of the seismic events has been told by many. Suffice to say that we now live in a significantly damaged city that will take decades to repair and rebuild. Although the local people have been resilient, the earthquake has had a marked effect on those living in the city and the surrounding areas.

For us, there has been the loss of places that were home to special memories. The restaurants Paul and I went to on our first dates were demolished. The church we were married in has a question mark over it at this point. It is likely to need major repair work. Our wedding reception venue is gone, as is the place where we stayed for our wedding night.

Some of our friends lost their homes to the earthquake. I knew some of those who lost their lives.

Paul spent months working from home. Since then, he has moved from place to place for office space.

On a personal level, my look towards the future is now one that is filled with many questions, including where my family might be in the years ahead. Looking back over the years, though, I am acutely aware of the fingerprints of God on our lives. He has given us amazing gifts over the years: a wonderful marriage, two fantastic kids, an interesting church family, a home, and jobs.

Looking back, I know with absolute assurance that even when things are incredibly black and dark, nothing separates us from God's love. Even when everything seems impossible, God is leading us through it. I know that even though things happen that scare me and hurt me, whether it be abuse, ill health, the health problems of people whom I love, or even earthquakes, God, in his mercy, plants courage in my heart. He has made us all to be overcomers.

One thing is for sure: the amazing, awesome God of heaven is an interested participant in our lives. I am sure that he will continue to be so.

Are You Walking a Similar Path?

My Dear Friend,

You may be one of the people reading my story who will find similarities between my story and your own. Depending on where you are on your journey, this book may have touched some sensitive areas for you.

Back when I was working very hard to rewire my thinking, I was desperate to know that there really was a way through all the pain and hurt. My message to you is this: there is great pain in life, but there is also healing and wholeness beyond the pain.

I am sorry that there is pain of any type, but I am particularly sorry that there is pain delivered from the hands of one person to another. I am so sorry that your life has been touched by this kind of pain.

It can be very difficult to see past the pain to anything else. I know that for me, the pain and the darkness around me seemed never-ending and overwhelming. But hear me when I say that there is an end to it and you really are stronger than you think.

Of course, the event that caused your pain will always be part of your story. It may even be a significant part of your story. However, there are pages of your story still to be written. There is the opportunity for the next chapters of your story to shine with the amazing healing and restoration that God has worked in your life.

Looking back now, I see that one of the things that made a huge difference to me was having support. The man who abused me took a great deal of effort to isolate me in order to ensure that I would keep quiet about his actions. It took great courage for me to reveal what had happened, but, in all honesty, it took even more courage for me to reach out to people and to allow them to support me. I had become very self-reliant, but this really was too big for me to handle on my own. Even now, it still takes courage to share my story.

There is something you should understand, though. Not everyone will understand your story or its impact on your life. Don't be discouraged. Remember that what matters is that you have a journey to take, starting from a position of hurt and pain and moving through to a place of healing and wholeness. Caring friends and family who will support you can make a massive difference. There will be people who understand where you have come from and where you are heading.

Having the help of some very skilled professionals made a huge difference for me. People who understood what had happened to me and the implications of that history to my life, made a huge difference for me. I appreciated their skills. They knew when to push me hard (and yes, I did need pushing hard at times) and when to give me space to take a big breath before carrying on. They were able to help me see the bigger picture and, thus, to see a way through it all.

Just so you know, they were also lovely people and they genuinely cared for me. I do think that there was an additional understanding between Peter and me, which was probably because we share a faith in God. He was able to talk me through my faith-related questions. He could be very direct when doing so!

You will need to work with someone that you trust and that you get along with. The process is tough enough without battling with the counsellor! But I warn you, no matter who you are working with, there will be things said that you will not like. Hang in there.

It will be really important for you to keep in place the things that are important to you and the things that you enjoy. If you run, then keep running. If you love movies, then keep watching movies. If you like to dance, then keep dancing. If you play a sport, then keep playing the sport.

More than anything, however, it is vital to keep the faith. Working through your history and healing the damage can take a real toll on your faith – and doesn't the Enemy just love that? Hear me when I say that some times will be tougher than other times. Keep going to church even when you don't feel like it. It is my observation that the hardest service to miss is the first. The more that you miss, the easier it becomes not to go to church. Just being in church and around God's people is good for your heart and for your healing. It isn't necessary for everyone to know what you are facing. You don't need to wear your heart on your sleeve. But do find two or three people who will pray with you and for you regularly.

Talk to God. Simple, huh? Just talk to him. Tell him how you feel. Tell him what you think or what you are struggling with. For me, it was so very releasing when I was told that my God is big enough to cope with my feelings – even when I am angry!

Read the Bible, as it really does help. I spent a long time reading the book of Psalms – at times, I read only Psalms – repeatedly. The way King David described his angst was so very familiar to me and I found it so helpful when David would flip from expressing his angst to offering extravagant praise of God.

Listen to music, especially worship music or music with scriptural lyrics. I found that I needed to be careful about listening to anything that was too melancholic and certainly not too much of it.

Let me encourage you to get out there and to keep mixing with people. It would be so easy to hide away, but it can make a huge difference to how you feel to be spending fun time with friends. Push yourself to go out even when you don't feel like it. Somehow, just being out and about helps you to feel better about yourself and about life.

I would like to give you a firm word about looking after yourself. It is fairly easy for people who have been abused to fall into risky behaviours that are only going to risk causing you more harm.

That means to go easy on alcohol. Some people use alcohol to anaesthetise their emotional pain, but its effect is very temporary and you risk experiencing all the negative effects associated with alcohol use. It must be noted that alcohol has a depressant effect. It will lower your mood further.

As for illicit or recreational drugs, the dangers of using these are high and their use is certainly not going to help you to arrive at a healthy place. Simply put, just don't go there.

Guard your heart, especially until it is healthy and whole again. Sexual relationships hold some appeal to those of us who are desperate to feel loved, special, and wanted. But once again those casual sexual relationships will cause more injury and hurt. There are those ready to take advantage of you, who will tell you what you want to hear in order to satisfy themselves. Guard your heart and wait. I know that it sounds cliché, but wait for the right person to appear at the right time.

Remember to take things a day at a time. Some days will be easier, and the distance back to what happened to you and today will seem much bigger. Always celebrate your success and progress. Be encouraged by it! Write it down and date it so that you can remind yourself of it later.

Other days will be tougher. These days can seem bleak and endless, but those days also end. Things will improve again soon.

Do remember that when things seem black, you need to keep talking and praying. There will be someone with whom you can be completely honest about how you are feeling. Please make sure that you do talk with this person.

The Psalms tells us that "his mercies are new every morning." and I firmly believe that each morning brings the mercies that are needed for that day. Even though we might not feel it, God's provision of mercy is there, ready for you every morning.

Always remember who you are and by that I guess that I mean that it is important to remind yourself of how God sees you. The best antidote to the poison dripped over your life by an abuser is to hear how your Heavenly Father sees you and to know how he cares for you.

Here, let me start you off with some thoughts:

- *He knew you before you were born, and he knows you very well (Psalm 139).*
- *He chose you before the creation of the world (Ephesians 1:4).*
- *He loves you, and his love endures forever (Psalm 118:2).*
- *He delights over you with singing (Zephaniah 3:17).*

I pray that as you walk this journey, you will know and experience the presence of God going with you.

I pray that God would surround you with skilled people to support you on your way.

I pray that God would heal your heart and your mind so that you can walk into a life of wholeness.

I pray that God would provide his light for you in the darkest of days. I pray for his protection over your precious life, especially in the darkest moments.

I pray that God will fill your heart with hope – his hope for the amazing life that is ahead of you.

I pray that God will bless you with discernment, wisdom, and perseverance for the work ahead.

I pray that God would bless you with a sense of humour amongst the sadness and the grief, because "a merry heart doeth good like a medicine" (Proverbs 17:22).

I pray that God would grant you the ability to see yourself as he sees you. I pray that you will have an increasing awareness of how very special you are to God. He is the Creator of the universe and he calls you friend.

I pray that you will see the fingerprints of a loving God all over your life too.

With much love,

Suzanne

When a Family Member or Friend Is on a Similar Path

Dear Friend,

O the heartbreak of caring for and supporting someone who has been through the pain of abuse and recovery.

It is well worth remembering that your perspective on the situation and on the person's place in their recovery might be very different from the person themselves. Frequently, those who are supporting people who are in the midst of a recovery process are more quickly able to see the enormity of the situation and the evil of the thing that has happened.

First, remember that you will have your own emotional reaction to the situation. You may well be faced with your own anger, disgust, anxiety, disbelief, frustration, and even guilt. These feelings will be even stronger if you know both the victim and the perpetrator. Resist any temptation to explain or justify what has happened. The ugly incident will sit very uncomfortably in your mind and your heart, which is as it should be.

It is vital that you understand the abused person's need to be safe and to feel safe. Please ensure their safety and protect them from having contact with the abuser. Be very wary of taking sides. Don't pass messages from one to the other.

In amongst everything that goes on in these situations, you need to look after yourself. Maybe you will be able to process your own thoughts and feelings or maybe you will have a friend, colleague, or pastor who can support you as indeed you support the victim. Please be open to the idea that it can be very helpful for you to talk things through with a professional counsellor.

Do remember that no matter who you are talking to about the situation and your reaction to it, it is essential to be loyal to the loved one that you are supporting. Do not gossip it about him or her. Be so very careful where you discuss things and with whom you discuss them. So much harm could be done to the person you are caring for and, indeed, to the whole situation when care is not taken about where you are discussing the matter and with whom. Be particularly mindful of this in smaller cities and in church circles. It is easy for rumours to spread like wildfire and the last thing that your loved one needs to be contending with is a wildfire!

Healing and recovery from any abuse is a long process. There will be moments of great joy when you see progress being made, but there will be moments of immense frustration when you will just want to remove their pain and the struggle. When you want things to be right. Moments where it all seems endless and hopeless. Hold on tight and know that there is a way through it all.

Healing does bring about great change to a person. Remember to encourage the positives. "I love how confident you were in that situation" and "It is great to see you so excited about doing that."

A history of being abused might explain a person's behaviour and reactions. In time, with help and healing it will not hold someone back at all. It cannot be used as an excuse for bad behaviour, but the bad behaviour may well indicate that there is a need for more help and healing.

There will be times when you will feel pushed aside and cold-shouldered. It is not personal. Hang around and remain available to the person, but be careful not to demand too much from him or her at this point. Things will change. Sometimes, just your being available without making any demands is very valuable. Loving silence can mean very much.

A big part of you will want to protect them and to stop them hurting. There will be hurt. and you cannot stop that hurt. As I said previously, ensure that they are safe from further abuse or harm. There are other ways that you can help guard them – be mindful of what is being watched on the television or at the movies. For me I still do not tolerate violent programmes or movies. And while I do enjoy a good mystery, my lovely family and husband understand that programmes (even documentaries or news items) about the abuse of children will be too much for me. Fortunately, the television comes with a remote which has an off button. Use wisdom and discernment when selecting books to read.

You need to be so very protective of your hope – both for yourself and for the loved one for whom you are caring. Recovery is long and hard, but it is significantly harder when one has no hope. Sometimes for the person who is in the middle of the storm (in fact any type of storm), it can be extremely difficult to see a way ahead or to find the light at the end of the tunnel. Please hear me say that there is light at the end of the tunnel and there most certainly is a way through to the end of the dark times. Hear the hope and remember to share the hope – even when they do not seem to hear you or want to believe you.

There will be times when you need space. That is okay, but remember that it is best to explain to your loved one that you'd like time alone. It would be very easy for your distance to be interpreted as rejection or punishment.

It is okay not to know quite what to do or know what the person needs. They may not know what they want or need either! Ask them what they would like to do, or rattle off some suggestions – a hug, a shopping trip, a walk around the park, a funny movie.

Just one note of caution: if the person who has been abused is in counselling, then leave the counselling to the professional. Be respectful of that relationship. You do not need to know what is being discussed. Your role in this is simply to encourage the person you love to see the work through.

I pray that there will be an amazing work of healing in your loved one's life, carried out by the Creator's own hands. I pray that you will see ever so clearly his fingerprints on your loved one's life. I pray that you will have an amazing relationship that reflects the awesome healing that has been worked.

Most of all, I pray that God would grant you great wisdom, abundant patience, and a timely sense of humour.

May God be with you all, and may you be aware of his presence as you make this journey together.

Yours in Christ,

Suzanne

So, You Are Pastoring Someone with a similar Story to Mine

Congratulations!

I personally believe that God carefully selects those who will shepherd those amongst his flock who are bruised and wounded.

My experience is that God selected the right people to be in the right place at just the right moment. Sure, I made decisions about which churches I would attend and so on, but very clearly I had encounters with key people along the way. In particular were those people in pastoral care positions. Don and Ruth were absolutely the right people at the right time for me. Their encouragement and support (and even correction!) were absolutely priceless.

It is worth noting that in countries like New Zealand, there are a significant number of women or girls who are sexually abused or sexually assaulted. I have heard the figure quoted that as many as one in three girls or women are sexually abused or sexually assaulted (and, of course, a significant number of boys). Statistically, these people are likely to be represented amongst your flock.

Trust me: it is not always obvious who they are. When I think back and remember the churches that I have been part of and all the people who have been leaders in those churches, I realise that there were only four people (amongst the pastors or church leaders) who knew anything at all of my story. That is a small number given the length of time it took me to work through counselling. Even in the intervening years, there really are only another two or three people in leadership positions with whom I have shared my story. As I said previously, in general there are not many people that I have shared my history with — until now.

In my humble opinion, the ongoing sexual abuse or sexual assault of girls and women has implications on how we live out our church life. It affects the following things:

- *How we regard women*
- *How we talk to women*
- *How we listen to women*
- *How we respect women (or not)*
- *How we teach girls and women, especially about dating or marriage*
- *How we counsel girls and women*
- *How we preach*
- *How we provide small-group settings*
- *How we try to exert authority*

There is another challenge, though, and that is how are we training our boys and men to treat girls and women. I see a need for the church and, indeed, for Christians to take a lead in how we treat our own people and others in the community. There is a need for the Christians to rise up and say, "This is not right. It is unacceptable. There is a better way to relate to one another." I offer my salute to those who are actively involved in putting a stop to human trafficking around the world. This a a major issue on a global scale and Christians need to be at the forefront of a movement to rescue these girls and women. Christians need to be working to put protections in place to prevent trafficking happening. There is a danger in viewing the enormity and the seriousness of human trafficking to overlook the damage being done to girls and women closer to home. We must not minimise those behaviours and their effects. We must remember the vulnerable members of our own communities.

First things first: in our individual Christian walks, we are all aiming for maturity. The apostle Paul encourages us to move on in our faith – from drinking milk to eating meat. "When I was a child, I spoke like a child, I thought like a child, I reasoned like a child. When I became a man, I gave up childish ways" (1 Corinthians 13:11).

Surely in any Pastoring setting, our goal is to enable people to mature spiritually. Our intention is not to create a people that are immature and dependent on the leader. Instead, our intention is to encourage them to be people of maturity – interdependent, able to discern, able to weigh up the Scriptures for themselves – and people growing in the fruit of the Spirit.

We are all in need of Christ's forgiveness. When he heals us – when we first become aware of our need for a Saviour – is when we first meet him. Of course, our need for forgiveness and healing continues throughout our Christian walk.

For those amongst the flock who have significant hurts, the process of healing can be ongoing. It usually is. It can take some time, considerable time, for a person with these hurts to heal.

You need to be aware that the steps towards healing cannot be pushed or rushed. As Mohammad pointed out to me at one point, my flashbacks were a sign that there were things at the surface that were ready to be dealt with. My experience is that things come to the surface in the order in which I need to see to them, and generally at a time when I am able to deal with the next bit. It would be wrong (and, in fact, harmful) to push things faster or according to someone else's agenda when you are working with someone who is recovering from a traumatic experience.

Some of my favourite personalities in the Bible are people who experienced significant struggles. They serve as examples of how to walk in faith while the storms rage all around.

Elijah – what a man of God! He saw God work through him in miraculous ways and he heard the voice and mind of God repeatedly. We see the amazing scene atop Mount Carmel where God reveals his awesome power (and humiliates the prophets of Baal at the same time). Then we read that Jezebel threatens Elijah, who then flees into the wilderness, we see that things look so bleak to Elijah that he asks to die. He sleeps under a tree and is awakened by an angel who provides him with food and water. After doing this a second time, the angel tells Elijah what he is to do next.

I have always been struck by God's treatment of Elijah. He didn't lecture him or condemn him or kick him when he was down. He cared for him – gave him rest, water, and food. He gave him clear instructions about what to do next. He restored him. Elijah didn't exactly fade away quietly or disappear. He was again used as God's spokesman. Then he was welcomed home to the Father in a blaze of glory – or, more specifically, a chariot of fire.

Jonah, who was very naughty (and yes hurt people and could be difficult, obstinate, defiant, and rebellious), was told clearly what God wanted him to do (i.e. he was given some enviably clear guidance), but he didn't want to do it. He tried to do the opposite. Eventually (via the belly of a large fish), Jonah did what God had asked him to do. The result was perfect and was just what God had desired: the people of Nineveh heard the message and repented. But Jonah sat outside Nineveh and sulked. God provided a vine (a very-quick-growing one) for Jonah to use as shelter. Then God provided a teaching moment as a very hungry bug ate the vine. God didn't simply leave Jonah to it; he cared enough for Jonah to teach him.

Where am I going with this? Sometimes we Christians can be incredibly hard on those who are struggling. Many times in the New Testament, we are instructed on how to care for each other. The bar is set very high.

- *"Love one another" (John 13:34).*
- *"Be devoted to one another" (Romans 12:10).*
- *"Outdo each other in showing honour" (Romans 12:10).*
- *"Live in harmony with one another" (Romans 12:16).*
- *"Don't judge one another" (Romans 14:13).*
- *"Build each other up" (Romans 14:19).*
- *"Instruct one another" (Romans 15:14).*
- *"Make each other welcome" (Romans 15:7).*
- *"Care for each other" (1 Corinthians 12:25).*
- *"Bear each other's burdens" (Galatians 6:2).*
- *"Forgive one another" (Ephesians 4:32).*
- *"Submit to one another" (Ephesians 5:21).*
- *"Teach and correct one another" (Colossians 3:16).*
- *"Encourage each other" (1 Thessalonians 4:18).*
- *"Build up one another" (1 Thessalonians 5:11).*
- *"Seek to do good to one another" (1 Thessalonians 5:15).*
- *"Confess your sins to one another" (James 5:16).*
- *"Pray for one another" (James 5:16).*
- *"Show hospitality" (1 Peter 4:9).*
- *"Serve one another" (1 Peter 4:10).*

And yet it is too easy to convey that Christians don't have problems or to suggest those in need should just give their worries to Jesus. We may be nice to the person for a while and then expect him or her to pull up his or her socks and get on with things. In a case like this, our underlying message is, "I'm not interested in what is happening in your life."

For those who are bruised and hurting, healing can take a long time. Sometimes it will seem that a recovering person takes one step forward only to take two steps backwards. Be patient! Remember: "Count it all joy, my brothers, when you meet trials of various kinds, for you know that the testing of your faith produces steadfastness. And let steadfastness have its full effect, that you may be perfect and complete, lacking in nothing" (James 1:2–4). Maybe the lesson in patience might be for you as well as the person in the midst of the storm.

So what can you do?

- Pray. This sounds simple, but never underestimate the power of prayer, especially in long, drawn-out battles or struggles. Pray for peace. Pray for healing. Pray that the individual will have a greater awareness of the love of God. Pray that the person will have godly appointments with the right people at the right time. Pray for protection for his or her life, because some really are in a battle for their lives. Pray for specific things, like an end to the person's nightmares. Breakthroughs in specific areas are a great encouragement. Pray when you see the person at church or just in passing. If the person comes to mind, pray. When someone mentions the person, pray.
- Mind your tongue! My mother used to say, "If you can't say something nice, then don't say anything at all." There is something in that. It is okay not to know the right thing to say. Sometimes a smile and a nod of the head is enough to indicate that you are on the same team as the person who is hurting.
- Now, really watch your tongue! It is very easy in Christian circles to gossip by sharing information. For example: "We need to pray for [so-and-so] because [of this or that problem or situation]." Always ask permission before sharing information about the person's history or struggle. It is his or her story to share or not. There is only one exception to this rule – and that is when you have cause to believe the person's life is at risk or that abuse is ongoing for this person. Then you must speak to the appropriate people. Who that is will depend on the

circumstances. It may be the person's General Practitioner, the police, or Child, Youth, and Family Services – or someone else.

- *Encourage the person. Don't make this traumatic part of his or her life the only topic of conversation that you have with them and don't avoid the individual! I know that people who are hurting can be hard work – I'm sure that I was! Compliment them on their progress and their hard work. Remind them that there is a light at the end of the tunnel.*

- *Build the person into a network. It is very easy for someone who was abused to withdraw or to feel unworthy. Encourage others to interact with them. Encourage him or her to join a group or to serve in some way.*

- *Build yourself a network. Find some godly health professionals (trained counsellors, psychiatrists, psychologists, or mental-health nurses), people who can answer your questions and people who can help you debrief.*

- *Be practical. Okay guys, let's think this through. It may not be appropriate or helpful for you to see this person on a one-to-one basis. Is your wife (or husband) or someone else available? Be aware that while you may feel comfortable, it doesn't mean that the other person is! Be aware of touching or hugging a person who has been sexually abused (or anyone in actual fact). A touch or a hug may mean nothing in particular to you, but it may be excruciating for someone who has been abused. I remember one chap who would insist on hugging me. There was nothing in it – he hugged everyone. It was agony for me, however. I took to carrying around armfuls of things so as to provide a barrier between me and that person.*

- *Don't go there! Being available to provide spiritual guidance and support to an abused person is one thing, but my advice would be to leave the counselling to those who are trained.*

Apart from anything else, too many fingers in the pie are only going to make things messy.

- *Make yourself aware of the resources available to someone who is struggling. What is there in your own church community, in the wider church community, or in the wider community of your town or city? God used Christians and non-Christians in my walk towards healing. He did pick excellent people!*

Remember that ultimately it is God's work in a person's life that brings healing and wholeness. Our role is to aid hurting people by providing an environment for them that is nurturing and caring.

It is truly wonderful to have a front-row seat to watch as God works in someone's life. To see his amazing transforming work is very humbling.

I pray that God would bless you with great empathy and compassion for all of the sheep in the flock that he has entrusted to you.

I pray that God would open your eyes to see the wounds of the injured sheep in your flock – whatever injuries they might have. I pray that God would open your eyes to see these people as he sees them.

I pray that God will fill your heart with love so that you are able to love, bear, forgive, and encourage those who are injured amongst your flock and community. I pray that your church will be known as a safe place to be and a place of healing.

I pray that God will provide you with discernment so that you will understand the sometimes complex situations facing you. That he would grant you the right words to say in each situation.

I pray that God will bless you with amazing resources so that you lack for nothing in your task of tending to his flock.

I pray that God would prompt your heart to provide protection for those in your flock. I pray that you would hear the Holy Spirit's alarm bells alerting you to the wolves in sheep's clothing who would seek to damage and hurt your flock, especially those who are vulnerable.

I pray that God will bless your flock and that you will see God's amazing transforming works in the lives of your flock – particularly in the lives of those who are wounded. I pray that you will declare the amazing works of our awesome God.

Printed in the United States
By Bookmasters